To One of
The Best, Esté
love Dekker.
Shelley xx

I'm A Street Girl Now

Shelley Dekker

authorHOUSE®

AuthorHouse™ UK Ltd.
500 Avebury Boulevard
Central Milton Keynes, MK9 2BE
www.authorhouse.co.uk
Phone: 08001974150

© 2010 Shelley Dekker. All rights reserved.

No part of this book may be reproduced, stored in a retrieval system, or transmitted by any means without the written permission of the author.

First published by AuthorHouse   9/24/2010

ISBN: 978-1-4520-4611-2 (sc)

This book is printed on acid-free paper.

For Auntie Janie

Acknowledgements

To Bryan for always saying I could write this, love you.

To Rob, many thanks for all you help.

I'm A Street Girl

As the icicle droplet decides to drop from the rim of my hat, landing on the warmth of my neck, dithering there for only a moment before descending down to what little warmth remains on my back, I feel a sudden shudder through my whole body. I swear, I have given up the idea of trying to hold an umbrella along with my clipboard and all my paperwork. It's all too much. And anyway, the wind continues to blow so hard that if I turn to look in a different direction, my umbrella gets turned inside out, looking nothing like the way the manufacture intended it to.

A women in her mid thirties rushes past me in a bid to get out of the rain. Her shoes are of good quality. *Must be A B C1s*, I think, *just what I need*. I step towards her, but she's running too fast, and she's gone before I get a chance to say "Good morning, madam." I'm left with my I.D. card dangling redundantly from my clipboard. I don't like my I.D. card. The photo of me makes me look as if I have been on *Crime Watch* for at least a bank job, or spent a lifetime on illegal substances which have now taken their toll. It doesn't do the job it's supposed to and make me look like a nice person who is going to ask you to give me your name, address, telephone number. Doesn't make me look as if you could trust me with this information – let alone some of the other questions I might ask.

"Would you mind telling me which of these you have in your home? A DVD player, a CD Player, a plasma screen television?"

Seriously, would I give this information to someone standing on the street armed with a £1.99 clipboard with a dubious photo of themselves? No, I don't think so. But maybe someone will take pity on a middle-aged woman wrestling her umbrella in the rain. I shake my head.

If I don't get someone in the next five minutes I'll stop for a coffee, try to thaw out a bit, maybe then the smile will work the way it's supposed to.

"You poor thing, what are you doing today?" I hear the small voice behind me. I turn and see Alice. She's a regular. One of our groupies.

"Oh Alice, how are you my love?" I ask genuinely pleased to see her.

"Oh you know, not too bad. Weather's been playing my old bones up, but mustn't grumble. Just thought I'd pop into town, get a few bits. Anything I can help you with?" She looks down at my clipboard, pulling her scarf around her to keep the rain from doing the same to her as it's been doing to me all day.

"No darling. We're looking for gentleman today," I lie. "But it's always lovely to speak to you." I say this last part truthfully. Alice's a real sweet old girl, always ready with a smile.

"Well, don't get too cold." Alice smiles as she taps me on my arm before turning toward Marks and Spencer.

"See you darling." I shout after her.

A smile crosses my face as I remember the first time I met Alice. It was around the time I started this job, unaware of what fun and games lay before me, not knowing about people like Alice.

It had been one of those warm summer days with a haze about it. Standing approximately in the same location as I was today, clip board at the ready, I can remember seeing a rounded elderly woman approaching me. She was clutching four carrier bags, all of them seeming to have at least four or five pounds of potatoes in each of them. Little did I know at the time that it *was* potatoes in them.

Her eyes focus on me, a slightly troubled look crossing her face. She was heading straight for me, stopping a few yards before reaching me to adjust the weight from those awkward carrier bags before quickening her pace until she stood directly in front of me, making eye contact without hesitation. I remember noticing how clear and bright those shiny blue eyes stared into mine, giving no evidence of her true age. There was a concerned look about her.

"My dear, could you help me?" she had asked in a slightly posh voice, throwing my already perceived expectations of her which I had taken from her clothing. I noted the faded floral skirt, shabby woollen jumper with leather patches at the elbows, grey ankle socks which just peaked out above the well worn plimsolls which I imagined she had owned as a young girl, needing them for country dancing at school. She also had on a straw hat with the deepest purple flower springing to life from its edge.

"Yes if I can." I replied, having difficulty removing my stare from those spectacular clear eyes

"It's my bra" Alice continued without flinching "Seems to be a bit tight. Don't suppose you could undo it?"

"Uh, uh, yes," was all I could manage, my mind racing.

Is this a wind up, I wondered. *Is my supervisor or one of my fellow colleagues lurking somewhere to see how I'll react. Is this some sort of a test? Or am I being filmed on Candid Camera?*

"Still think I'm a size 10. Must have done it up to tightly this morning," Alice added without noticing my embarrassment. "If you could just unhitch me…"

I began to fumble with the tail end of the thick woollen jumper, working my way up her back, undoing the restricting garment. "Oh that's so much better, my dear, thank you so very much."

"That's OK," I heard myself saying as I looked round to check I wasn't on any security camera, headlines racing through my mind. "Elderly women sexually harassed by woman with clip board – I.D. photo confirmed woman was on crime watch last week."

"I've done the same thing myself," I stuttered

"Have you? We're silly things aren't we." Alice's smile broadened "Should have gone and sorted myself out before buying all these spuds from the market, but you know how it is when you see a bargain."

I found myself thinking, *When were potatoes expensive?*

Alice then went on to tell me the price she'd paid for her heavy load, how lovely the market trader had been giving her an extra pound of spuds due to her bulk purchase. She told me that her son was from Newmarket, and that he lives there now and would be visiting this weekend. She said how much he looked forward to her special roasties, his wife not being capable of doing them the same way Alice did. It was all to do with the temperature of the fat, she told me, and that secret ingredient salt, only to be added at the end of the roasting.

"Well I've held you up for long enough dear," Alice ended "Do you need any help with you work today?"

I was thrown totally, forgetting in the warm summer sun why I was standing there, lost in the intensity of our conversation, in Alice's natural warmth, her genuine personality, and those compelling eyes.

"Only I help a lot of the girls from time to time. Are you looking for my age group? Sometimes I fit. My name's Alice," she said trying to hold out her hand for me to shake, but only managing to raise it a few inches with the weight of those bargain spuds.

"Lovely to meet you, Alice." I fumbled looking at my quota, "How old are you?"

"I'll be sixty five in August," Alice said with pride.

"Sixty five," I said as if to make it true. "Well you don't look it."

"Yes, never used any of those beauty products." There was pride within her voice. "Had a good man to look after me for forty five years, put it down to that." Alice's eyes seemed to sparkle more than I thought possible. "He's still with me every single day, but not everyone believes that," she said with a wink. "Anyway can I help or not?"

"Well, Alice, we're looking for ladies up to 50 years old today."

"Oh that's alright my dear. Maybe some other time."

I could see she was disappointed.

"Yeah, that would be lovely, Alice." I added

"Well had better press on. Still got to go into Marks. Lovely to meet you, my dear. Are you new? Haven't seen you before?" she said with a grin.

"Yes, this is my first week."

"Oh you'll do fine. I can always tell. Anyway, must be off. Thanks for helping me out." She said turned to walk away.

"Bye" I said as she moved off toward what I was later to find out was her favourite shop, Marks & Sparks. "Lovely talking to you."

Alice never asked me to undo her bra again, but on the odd occasion would maybe ask me to adjust her hats, which varied with the seasons. Sometimes she'd be wearing the straw hat I'd first seem, with maybe a different coloured flower springing from the top of it, as if suspended in time. Sometimes she'd wear a deer stalker, never tied under her chin but flapping wildly about her ears, in extremely cold, windy condition. She might, on occasion, wear it with maybe a brightly coloured scarf under to add that bit of colour, this being so much a part of Alice's identity. Always the floral skirt in varying stages of fadedness, always the grey socks and plimsolls.

I like Alice. She always makes me feel better, encouraging me on even the worst days, saying she knows I'll do well. She makes me smile sometimes, and even laugh aloud at what she's told me she's been up to. I always look forward to our chats. Alice always has a story to tell, sometimes about the price of whatever she's bought, sometimes about her son. She's out and about in all weathers, telling me bits and bobs about her life, how she has had a full and loving marriage with Albert, obviously saddened by his sudden death, but believing they are always together. Her sparkling eyes never fail to transfix me.

I turn as another passer-by appears. "Excuses me Madam we're conducting a survey on…"

"You must be frozen!" the woman replies.

"Just a bit. Not the best of days to be doing this, is it? Don't suppose you'd like to take part in a survey about deodorant? We're looking for ladies to get their opinion on some recent advertising."

"Go on then, I'll do it. I've got a few minute to kill before I meet my mum."

"This is my I.D. card my names Shelley and I work for…"

This wonderful woman stands with me under the tiny amount of shelter possible to achieve from a local shop's sun blind, obviously put out by mistake given the weather conditions. In the freezing cold, with rain drizzling down, I ask her, "Do you strongly agree, disagreed, with this or that statement…" and we do the whole interview.

Taking the somewhat soggy thank you note from the company I work for, and a token pen at the end of the interview, I thank her.

"No not at all, I enjoyed it," She says, pulling the warmth of her winter coat around her to face the elements again, tucking away her fabulous new possession – a blue pen – into her handbag, "Hope you get on OK." she smiles.

"Thanks I really appreciate your time." I smile back.

"No probs, bye."

That's why I love this job. It's the people you have the privilege to meet. Would I work in an office or factory seeing the same faces nine to five? No. In this job you meet all walks of life, some distinctively odd, some run of the mill – all of them with their own story to tell. No day is the same. I have to laugh as I think of what my husband has dubbed my new career. I'm a street girl, working the streets. I'm now an official Market Researcher. It says so on my I.D.

Retired And Bored

How do you become a market researcher and why? Everyone's story is different. The market researchers I have worked with are all as different as the people we interview. They are from all walks of life. There is even a Lord of the Realm, working as a market researcher, although he preferred that fewer people know this fact about him, the better.

I can't say I ever remember my careers officer at school giving me the option, never remember them saying, "Well here's a job opportunity to look at. How about becoming a market researcher? You're out and about. Get to meet people. The added bonus is it's very flexible. You can work in all weathers, from extreme cold to blistering hot sunshine. Meet some of the loveliest of people, and also see the human race at its worst. Talk to some very rude people. By the way they're the ones you'll remember most out of the hundred or so you will speak to each day. Hear stories to make your hair curl, or make you laugh till it hurts. The pay's not bad. What do you think?"

The only options I recall being offered were bog standard jobs. But then I suppose in fairness if I'd been given the opportunity I would have turned it down aged seventeen. In truth, I probably wouldn't have had the confidence then, which you need to take the rejections. Nor would I have had the ability to make people feel at ease when asking them some of the personal questions which are sometimes part of the job. It was to be some thirty two years after leaving school that I went along for an interview, finding out for the first time about market research.

I wasn't looking for employment for myself, but had been scanning the local papers for a job for my youngest daughter who had returned after working for the summer season in Majorca as a holiday rep.

"This sounds as if it might do Jennie." I shouted through to my husband from the sitting room. "Hours to suit, outgoing personality, training given…"

Peter appeared in the doorway holding a fresh cup of tea. "What's it for?"

"Doesn't say."

"There's always one of those 'make money quick' ads every week," Peter said as he began to flick through the channels on the telly.

"It's quite a big ad. Must be a large company," I said, my stare returning to the centre of the page as I read the advert more carefully.

"Doesn't mean anything," Peter said, although his concentration was now with Trevor MacDonald, who was reporting on the latest house price increases.

"I'll just give her a ring. See what she thinks. There's one or two options in here." I had already picked up the phone dialling Jennie's number. She answered after three rings and I told her about the jobs I'd seen.

"Oh I don't know Mum, what do you think?"

"Well you need something till the next season." I tried to sound positive "This one doesn't sound too bad. Although Dad thinks it might be some sort of con."

"You come with me then." Jennie replied

"What? But I don't need a job. I've only just retired."

"Not for the job," Jennie groaned, "just to make sure it's OK. You know, just to make sure it's not a con like Dad says."

The thought of Jennie being conned made my smile. They'd have to get up very early to get one over on her, my bright wonderful, talented daughter who has a built in sense of weighing up any situation in all of five seconds.

"Anyway Mum, you're fed up with retirement," Jennie giggled

"I'm not," I said a bit too defensively.

"Oh come on Mum. You've been round to see us all twice this week and it's only Wednesday," Jennie laughed out loud. "Maybe you need a hobby or something?"

She was right, although I wasn't about to admit it, after working for Peter for the past twenty five years, in our family business, I had decided now that our other two kids had come to work for us that

I'd hang up my boots. I'd start enjoying myself, and take time to do the garden, visit friends, go to the leisure centre, and relax a bit. It had been fun for the first two months, lying in bed, getting up leisurely, pottering around. But now I was bored. I'd always hated gardening. It was a job when I was working we'd always had to fit in. Now I had all day to keep on top of it. Our garden was now so neat and tidy with the lawn standing at attention, not a blade of grass out of place. The visiting friend was good, but you can only sup so much coffee in any given day. Also if I was to be totally honest, my trips to the leisure centre became something I started to dread. Peter would ask if I'd gone for a swim, I'd make some lame excuses about not going, why I couldn't just admit that swimming up and down for an hour by myself wasn't enjoyable, not fun if you didn't have someone to share that time with. I now knew how many ceiling tiles covered the pool area and that there were fifty six small stains caused by the condensation. How sad was I becoming? Why was I still trying to kid myself into believing that being a "Lady of Leisure" was what I wanted?

Jo, our eldest daughter, had caught me pumping her cushions on the sofa when I'd popped round on Monday.

"Short of something to do, Mum?" Jo smiled at me as she came into the room.

"No, just making it look OK," I said as I purposely flopped into the chair as causally I could.

"Dad OK?" Jo asked as she sat on the sofa, making the cushions I'd so neatly rearranged moments before crumple and sag.

"Yes he's fine. You know Dad." My answer was half hearted, my mind concentrated on those cushions behind Jo. They needed to be straightened.

"Stop worrying about the cushions, Mum," Jo laughed. "You're turning into Nan."

"I'm not worrying," I said.

"You miss work, don't you?" Jo caught me by surprise with this question.

"No. What made you ask that?"

"Mum, you've never been one for doing nothing." Jo was suddenly serious. "Maybe you need a hobby or something."

"I'm still busy you know," I lied. "There's always something to do in the garden."

"You hate gardening," Jo laughed. "Anyway, the only way you could make that garden any neater would be to get the hoover out, then dust and polish the garden gnome."

Even I laughed at this statement. She was right.

"Why don't you go back to work for Dad? You could just do part time."

"No, Jo. I've done accounts for years. And anyway, it wouldn't be the same going back. Dad's pleased that I've retired and you're both working there now. It's what we've always planned. In a few years Dad will retire."

Jo and I both looked at each other, knowing each other's thoughts, giggles leaving us both. My darling Peter retired – what would we do then? Not only would the lawns look immaculate but the trees would pass a falling out parade any Squadron Leader would be proud of. Peter and I had built up our business. We weren't work alcoholics but it had been an uphill struggle over the years, and neither of us were work shy.

"Maybe you're right. Maybe I do need a hobby."

Later that evening, I was in the kitchen starting dinner when Jennie came in.

"Are you going to come with me to see if that job's a con or not?" she asked.

"Yes, I'll go with you," I said.

"Thanks. What date is it anyway?"

I glanced down at the newspaper on the counter. "It's on the 30th at the Guild Hall. Interviews start at 9.00 am sharp."

"OK, see you there. Sorry but got to go, Tom's coming round in five. Love you." With that, she was gone.

As I walked back into the sitting room Peter looked up.

"She going to go then?" he asked, not lifting his gaze from the telly.

"Yeah, and so am I."

"What?" Peter looked across at me

"She wants me to meet her there, just to check it's OK. Check it's not a con."

Peter smiled, "Jennie wants you to see if it's alright." He knew our daughter. "Well I suppose it'll be interesting."

"Umm," I mumbled, wondering what people these days wear to interviews.

The Interview

"What are you doing?" Peter turned over looking at me through sleepy eyes.

"Don't know what to wear. Do you think this'll do?" I asked, taking a fifth look at myself in the mirror. I turned to check the back view of my outfit hadn't changed in the last ten seconds.

Peter yawned, his mop of now greying hair flopping into his eyes. "Do for what?"

"The interview, silly. Do you think black is too severe? Maybe the blue?" I held the blue number against myself.

"The black's fine, for god's sakes. It's 6.30 in the morning, Shelley. How long have you been up?" Peter double checked the alarm clock beside the bed.

"Not long. So you think the black?" I looked at the jumble of clothes scattered at my feet.

"Looks like you've had your own little fashion show." Peter was now getting out of bed.

"Well I want to look right," I said, pursing my lips as Peter crossed the bedroom to kiss me.

"Thought it was Jennie who was having the interview?"

"Yes, but I don't want to let her down. It's the black then?" I checked one final time in the mirror. "Want breakfast?"

Peter smirked. "Maybe later. Still too early for me." He wrapped his arm around me and gave me a soft kiss on the neck. "What do you say we go back to bed?"

"Oh, you're a horny little devil," I giggled slipping from his bear hug. "But I have to get going. I can't let Jennie down."

"I guess I could manage some toast." Peter grinned.

I arrived at 8.30 and bought a coffee from Costa, giving myself a few moments to collect myself, and sit and wait for Jennie to arrive. Sipping the extremely hot coffee, I checked my watch again. It seemed Jennie would be late as usual.

I could feel a slight annoyance rising in me.

You'd think she'd be here on time if only to please me after I've gone to the trouble of finding this interview for her, I thought. *No doubt she'll turn the corner with seconds to spare and with the biggest of smiles on her face, those dimples deep in her cheeks. That's right. She'll breeze in and walk the interview in her matter of fact way, while I sit stewing about the whole procedure.*

My coffee cooled.

It's 8.50 now... Where the hell is she?

I felt my phone buzz. Fumbling in my handbag, cursing the fact that mobile phones are always so difficult to find, I fished it out and saw I had a text message.

"Running late c u in ther luv Jennie."

Oh God, this is her interview! What is she playing at? Jobs don't fall out of trees.

What was I supposed to say to her perspective employers?

"Well, I'm here and my daughter will turn up shortly. You'll love her. Everyone does. She'll be brilliant at this job. She'll be a real asset to your company – however you might have to live with the fact she'll possibly be late now and again, like today...'

Of course, their reply would naturally be, "Late? Why, that's no problem at all. Of course we'll employ her. If you say she's bright, then what does it matter if she has the occasional lie-in on company time? We don't mind that. We're liberal, after all. If it's the famous Jennie Harris we're dealing with, then that's good enough for us."

Not likely.

"Oh, I'll kill her." I said aloud, not realising that I had.

"Sorry?" A large man sitting to the right of me turned to face me.

"Umm sorry, thinking out loud. I was supposed to meet my daughter here. She's got an interview in there." I nodded toward the Guild Hall.

"You're here for the interview?"

"No, I'm not. My daughter is." I explained to him, then it turned out he was applying for the same job.

"Really?"

"Really," he said. "Didn't tell you a lot in the ad, did it. Guess we should be heading in. See what it's all about."

Without thinking I was following a stranger though the solid open oak doors, I listened as he asked the receptionist where the interviews were being held.

"Crosslet's," she said. "You go thought that door and then it's up stairs first on you right." She had a receptionist voice with just the right amount of annoying squeakiness, an obvious requirement for obtaining any receptionists job.

As we climbed the stairs, the big man turned to check I was still following behind, "This is my third interview this week. Getting the hang of it now," he grinned.

"This is my first in thirty years," I tried to sound jovial.

Before going through the door, I turned, checking to see if my long lost daughter was maybe bounding up the stairs behind me, but there was no sign of her.

There were six other people sitting around a large table with various bits of paper in front of them. All of them looked up as we entered the room. I smiled, I think, but I could feel the sides of my mouth twitching.

"Hello there." A woman of about my own age, dressed in a business suit held out her hand. "I'm Pamela. Can I get you both a coffee?"

"Yes, that would be lovely, black no sugar." I shook her hand, the words I was looking for, unable to leave the back of my voice box. 'I'm not here for any interview. It's my daughter you want to see. She's running a bit late…' Instead I smiled back at Pamela, taking a seat at the large table next to the friend I'd just made outside.

Looking round the table at my fellow interviewees, I suddenly felt quite overdressed. Everyone else had turned up in casual attire.

Maybe this is how people attend interviews nowadays, in jeans and fleeces. I'm no spring chicken myself, but all these people seem to be the wrong side of sixty – apart from a man who appeared to be in his late thirties.

My thoughts were interrupted as Pamela walked over with two cups of coffee. At least she'd come in a business suit.

"Black no sugar, and white with one." Pamela placed two coffee cups in front of me and third interview this week man. "Just waiting for a couple of other people, then we'll begin."

I looked down at the small pile of papers which must have been intended for Jennie but now for some reason belonged to me.

"Thanks," was all I managed.

Pamela glanced at her wrist watch, "Oh well, we might as well make a start."

I glanced over at the large oval clock hanging on the opposite wall: 9.05, and still no Jennie.

"Well I'm Pamela, maybe if I start by telling you a bit about Crosslets, then about Market Research. Then you can ask any questions you may have."

Pamela explain that Crosslet's had been started by two English men, but was now owned by an American Company, working both nationally and internationally. The Head Office was based in Northampton, and was, by all accounts, a massive place employing over 600 people, with over 3000 market researchers working in the UK alone. Support was given from Team Leaders and Supervisors, helping these market researchers do their job. Major companies would approach Crosslet's with new adverts and products which would be launched, or adverts of products that were already launched but were not achieving their targets. It was then the job of the 'Field Workers', otherwise known as market researchers, to then approach the public armed with a super-do-pa questionnaire, worded correctly, to find out either why the advert or product was not achieving, or what the general public would think of any new product or possible advert which would promote a new and exciting commodity. Crosslet's were second to none, giving two days full training, one of those being today. After that there would be a day in the 'Field' to see how we performed. If we did well at this, felt happy and able to cope, then the job was ours.

Pamela instructed us to look through the papers which were laid in front of us all. These gave fact and figure about Crosslet's in graph and diagrammed form. We all fumbled through these. I wasn't sure if mine were in the right order but did my best to look as if I knew what I was doing, glancing up every now and then to check that my companions round the table were on the same page as me, or if the truth be known, that I was on the same page as them.

Pamela told us Market Research isn't for everyone. She said you had to be able to take rejection – all the 'No's' when people declined to give their opinion. It didn't always take place on sunny summer days. You had to be able to face the elements. She explained that there are in place strict rules governing market researchers. There is a Code of Conduct. Some work is venue based, some worked from what Pamela called "Packs", neither of which meant anything to me.

I managed a couple of serious nods every now and then, hoping that they would convince Pamela's as well as myself, that I understood what she was talking about, noting that some of the my fellow interviewee's did the same.

Maybe they know more than me. Or maybe they're all trying not to look too stupid.

"Any questions?" Pamela asked.

"Wot's the pay like?" a rough sounding man asked sitting across from me.

Pamela looked over to the middle-aged chap and smiled. "It varies depending on the type of work you do, which I'll run through this afternoon."

"Yeah, but wot sort of pay rate are we talking?" I mean if we're got to stand out in all weathers and take abuse from every passer-by, must pay well."

"This sort of work isn't for everyone, as I said. If it's not something you'd be interested in doing, then you're free to leave."

Clever girl, I thought.

"Don't sound like much of a job to me," he said as he stood to leave.

"Thank you for coming along anyway." Pamela smiled back at him.

There was an uncomfortable silence as the man collected his belonging and left.

"Any one got any other questions?" Pamela asked, totally unfazed by the last few minutes.

"You mentioned Field and Venue work. Pamela, could you explain the difference as I'm not sure what it means?" I heard a confident voice say, realising it was my voice only because Pamela was now looking in my direction.

Pamela went on to explain that some surveys were based in a venue with a quota of different people to interview. Alternatively, you could be sent a pack of work which you worked either by going house to house, 'door knocking' as it was called, until you found the right sort of people. Or there was 'street work,' where you were sent to a location to work in the street of a city or town. Expenses were paid for your travelling time and petrol.

A couple of other people in the room asked a few questions, then it was suggested that we adjourned for lunch for half an hour.

"This afternoon," Pamela explained, "we'll run through a paper questionnaire while pairing up with each other. See how you cope with this next bit."

My colleague who was on his third interview this week walked down the stairs behind me.

"What do you think of it so far?" he asked.

"Well seems alright, don't really understand it all, but maybe it'll be a bit clearer this afternoon." I tried to sound unimpressed.

"Well you got to give it a go," he said. "Think that other bloke was a bit rash."

"Um, yeah," I agreed.

After a bit of lunch, I phoned Peter just to let him know I was alright. I also left a message for Jennie telling her she wasn't. Returning back to the Guild Hall, I found myself wanting to know more about this possible part time job. It seemed not only like something I could do, but also like something I could do well.

Perhaps I might just have found something to keep me busy.

My First "Excuse Me"

Peter listened to me carefully as I explained about my day. I told him about the middle aged man who had left the meeting and exactly what Market Research was – now that I was almost an expert! I told him how we'd all interviewed each other on what they called a Papi survey. "It's called Papi because it's done on paper," I told him, then I went on to tell him how they also did surveys on computers, describing the other interviewees and how we'd been a pretty mixed bunch.

"There was this really funny lady called Sally. She went completely to pieces when I paired up with her. Got every sentence back to front and circled the wrong responses. But Pamela said it was normal." The excitement in my voice obvious. "I think I was OK though. Made a few mistakes, but not too many. Tomorrow Pamela's sending us outside to do an interview for real."

As I looked at Peter, I saw a wide grin crossing his face.

"I'm going on a bit, aren't I…"

"No, Shelley. I was just thinking it lovely to see you this enthusiastic."

"Sorry. I suppose it's not such a big deal. But it was nice to feel…" My voice trailed off. "Well, it was nice to feel busy again, I guess."

"Sound like the type of thing you could do," Peter looked over to me. "But you don't have to do this Shelley if you don't want to. The most important thing is that you're happy."

I looked over at my husband of so many years. I struck gold the day I met him. He's supported me in everything I have ever wanted to do. He smiled at me and it was then I knew that he'd realised before me that I'd end up taking the job. He seemed to know that I needed a purpose in the workplace, and that retirement just wasn't for me at the moment.

"I know I don't have to do this Peter," I said. "And maybe I won't be any good at it. But it doesn't sound too taxing. Pamela says they only require a maximum of two days a week if that's all you want to do – which would suit me down to the ground. Tell you what, I'll take you out for dinner on my first weeks wages. How does that sound?" I asked as I walked over and kissed him on the cheek.

"Hmm, dinner. Well, it'd better be somewhere decent then." Peter kissed me back. "Spoke to Jennie yet?"

"No. Texted the little bugger, but got no reply. It's such a shame. This would have suited her down to the ground."

"Well she's her mother's daughter. Now, woman where's my dinner," he joked. "This job had better not affect your wifely duties."

9.00 am sharp, and I was second to arrive at the Guildhall. Pamela was there. She remembered that I took black coffee without sugar, which impressed me. Only four of the original group had turned up for the second day's training. Even third interview man didn't appear. I wondered if maybe he'd got one of the other jobs.

"Well it's not for everyone." Pamela said again, looking around.

I began to wonder if this statement meant more than Pamela was telling us. This was the tenth time she'd uttered these words.

First we ran through a slide show all about Crosslet's, detailing their aims and what they were about. My mind wandered elsewhere, concentrating on the "going outside to interview the public" bit of the training.

Oh God what if I'm rubbish at it? I began to worry. *What if I can't get anyone to stop?*

Getting myself into a momentary panic, I began to wondering what I doing here. I started thinking that the garden must need something doing to it. It had also been a whole day since I'd spoken to, let alone visited the kids. Maybe their cushions needed pumping…

What was I thinking of yesterday? Do I really need this hassle?

"OK we'll break for lunch, see you all at 1.30. Then we'll begin recruiting." Pamela said this without a care in the world.

Over my sandwich and coffee in the little Tea Room opposite the Guildhall, anxious thoughts flooded my head. I began thinking that I was being silly.

I've retired. What am I putting myself through this for? We don't need the money. I could be swimming lengths in the pool. Who cares about how many of the tiles have stains on them? I don't really need this job. If anything, I'm taking employment from someone who really needs it.

I felt the buzzing from my mobile in my coat pocket.

"Hello?"

"Just phoned to say I love you," I heard Peter's voice say. "Thought we'd try that new Italian restaurant with your first set of wages."

"What?"

"That new Italian restaurant," Peter laughed.

"Italian restaurant?"

"When you take me out as a kept man," he laughed again.

"Oh Peter, what if I can't do it?"

"Can't do what?"

"What if… What if I'm no good?"

"Shelley, I know you can. You can do anything if you really want to."

"But…"

"Listen, do you want me to come and pick you up?"

He would. I just had to say so.

"No. I'm just being silly, ignore the last two minutes. Italian it is!"

There was a second of silence.

"I love you Shelley. Now go knock 'em dead."

"Yeah," I agreed. "And I love you too."

Returning to the Guildhall, Pamela greeted me with a kindly smile, which suggested she knew how nervous I was.

"Worried about this afternoon?"

I found the calmness in her voice a bit irritating.

"Don't worry," she said. "Everyone always is. You'll be fine."

I mustered a very faint smile, but before I could say anything the rest of my fellow interviewees arrived back from their lunch break and we began again.

Pamela's instructions were simple: ask everyone, smile a lot, and once you've got someone to agree to come in, just do the interview. Couldn't be easier.

Standing outside with my brand new clipboard at the ready, the gentle autumn sun causing a haze on the slight damp pavement, I looked around at the passers-by, and without thinking, I heard my own voice.

"Excuse me, madam, sir, we're conducting a survey. Would you be interest in taking part in the study?"

The middle aged couple I had spoken to looked over in my direction, my smile now wider than the Grand Cannon.

"Wot's it about?" asked the woman, mildly interested .

"It's on consumer products and services," I said repeating the words I'd been told to say, hands shaking a little.

"Go on then. We've got a bit of time."

I lead them into the Guildhall. Sitting them down, I offered them refreshment, and as I did, I caught Pamela's eye and she winked at me. A wave of calm passed over my whole body. This was for me and Pamela knew it – and now, so did I.

Sorry I Can't

Market researchers are a very mixed variety of people, very much like the people we interview. Some work on a part time bases, as I do, for a bit of 'pin money,' while for others some the job provides their main source of income. Everyone has their own way of asking the public if they will take part in a survey. I find myself sometimes watching the different approaches we all have. All are very different – as unique as the interviewer themselves.

The Code of Conduct for Market Research is extremely strict. You must always introduce yourself, then the company you work for, showing your I.D. card to any member of the public you stop. Sadly the first thing they see after you speak to them is this gruesome passport photo. I swear, if someone could only invent a way of even slightly improving how those photos turn out, they would have my undying gratitude forever, plus the thanks from all the other market researchers out there.

After showing your I.D. card, you must assure all respondents (members of the public) that everything they tell you is totally confidential, and that no personal data is ever passed on.

Working on a venue based job and after a mornings recruiting on a bright summer's day, I began to get an attack of the giggles at my own way of recruiting, I heard myself saying, "Excuse me Ladies." Only it was coming out "Scuse me Ladies", making me sound as if I should have been in a episode of Harry Enfield's *Kevin and Perry*. The more I tried not to say my introduction in this manner the more it came out "Scuse me Ladies". "Get a grip," I told myself. "Go back to saying 'Good morning, madam'. So I tried again,

"Scuse me Ladies," I snorted at two very young girls.

The bewildered girls looked on as I fell about laughing, not being able to manage any further information. Tears streaming from my eyes, they walked off, glancing back at this peculiar woman holding her nose, snorting.

I still can't get over that members of the general public will stop, listen to what you have to say, and then commit twenty to twenty five minutes of their time to completing a survey on toothpaste or whatever. Would I have stopped before knowing how difficult it can be to recruit? No, I'd make some lame excuse then walk by.

The excuses can be catalogued. Market researchers hear them all several times a day. There are the smilers who try not to make eye contact with you but are unable to avoid you at some point. They smile back at you politely before declining to take part, blushing profusely, as they do. Then there's the growlers, mumbling something as they rush past you. Sometime I wonder if they say anything at all. It's almost a primeval grunting.

Then there's the bad credit risk. "Can't have one of those, got a bad credit rating," they say. This is because they think you're trying to sell them something. I am always astonished that they are telling a perfect stranger about their financial situation.

The roundabouters always make me smile the most. These people will go to huge lengths to avoid you.

The worst roundabouter I encountered was on a supermarket contract. Crossett's had won a large contract with a supermarket chain to survey people's reactions to the installation of large televisions in their super stores. Our job was to conduct surveys at the exits of the store and also the exit near the café. It was decided that the four interviewers attending would alternate positions during the day, taking an hour at the main exit then changing over to the exit at the café. My first hour was to be at the café exit catching people before they went into the store after having a cuppa or a bite to eat.

A couple of surveys completed, I realised that no one had noticed the giant tellies suspended above them, advertising promotions, etc. I spied a young man leaving his Formica topped table where he had enjoyed a full English breakfast for only £2.99. He avoided any eye contact with me, obviously aware of what I was doing. Clip board at the ready, I stepped forward to approach him, deciding to stop after two steps. His obvious fear of doing a survey became very apparent. Instead of walking from his wood finish Formica topped table towards the exit, he veered towards the end wall of the cafeteria. He placed his back against the wall, and with the palms of his hands either side of him, began edging his way round the room, looking somewhat like Spider-Man as he worked his way slowly round to the exit were I was standing, unable to take my eyes off him. He edged past me, slipping through a narrow gap between me and the wall. At first I thought he was being silly, joking with me, but then I caught sight of his eyes. The resemblance of a rabbit stuck in head lights was uncanny. The thought of doing a survey seemed as terrifying to him as open heart surgery would be to me. Still, I was unable to remove my glare, which had I thought would maybe have made him less afraid. Still edging his way around the wall, I noticed he was fast approaching the newspaper stand to the right of the café exit.

"Mind," was all I managed to get out as he crashed, falling into the newspaper stand.

Newspapers fell to the ground and the stand made a huge thud as it hit the floor. Staff ran to his rescue, picking up a very bewildered young man who was still intent on escaping from the scary woman, armed with not a sawn-off shotgun but a clip board. I managed to suppress my laughter until he had disappeared down the next aisle.

It didn't end there. My hour at the café exit passed without further incident, but then it was all change. Off I went to work my hour at the store exit. I saw the same man out of the corner of my eye. Packing his groceries neatly into bags, he looked up. I smiled, hoping to reassure him that I wasn't a mass murderer. The smile was wasted.

Gathering his collection of plastic bags, the man backed to the nearest wall, well large window that fronted the super store, and began edging his way along the large panels of glass, his palms making a squeaking sound as they slid across the clean surface. His full plastic shopping bags banged against the glass frontage and I feared that the weight of them might break one of the panels of glass. Stepping back, I tried to assure him I meant no harm.

At last, he was inches away from the exit. I breathed a sigh of relief for him. He was finally going to be free. Seeing the open door he turned and ran.

Then an ear splitting alarm rang out through the whole store and out of nowhere two security guards ran over to apprehend him, each clasping his arms tightly. Frog marched back to the nearest check out, Spider-Man was asked to empty the contents of his plastic bags. Shoppers looked over, shaking their heads in disgust. Cashiers turned in their swivel chairs, mildly interested. The burly security guards checked through the purchases: a bottle of whisky had been purchased in a posh presentation box. Upon checking this it was found that the security tag attached to the bottle inside had not been removed, although the item had been paid for. This oversight by the cashier had caused the alarm to trigger. Apologise were made, and the bags were packed in regimental form. I felt somehow responsible, and wonder if I should I say something to this young man. In the end I thought better of it. I'd done enough damage with my clipboard. Maybe he had learnt a valuable lesson. A simple "No, sorry, haven't got time" would have done in the first place.

Teenage girls are a personal pet hate of mine. Getting them to stop, or even acknowledge you, especially if they are in pairs or groups, is nearly impossible. You approach this strange age group as you would anyone else, only to be rejected by them looking at each other and doing this awful giggle. There is never a reply to you. I guess I would have reacted similarly when I was their age – but then again, maybe not. I think I would have at least said *something*. Given the times we live in, some parents could have instructed their young vulnerable daughters not to talk to strangers. It's a possibility, but I'm not convinced. Groups of teenage girls remain a mystery to me.

There is another group known as the confessionals. These folk give you their life story as an excuse for not doing a survey. In the time they have given you a reason for not taking part they could have completed two, maybe at a push three, surveys.

Then there are the originals. These are excuses we as market researchers haven't heard before. A colleague of mine had one of the best when she approached a middle-aged woman.

"Excuse me, madam. We're conducting some market research…"

"Sorry luv, can't stop got to get home to look after my Cockatoo's."

Another favourite of mine happened when the same interviewer as she tried to stop a member of the public, only to get the reply, "My doughnuts will melt." Guess she couldn't argue with that one.

The lost in timers are these poor souls who don't seem to know what time of day it is. At ten-thirty on any morning they'll say they're on lunch. Maybe they're a shift worker. Maybe not. But a simple no would do. Mums seem to collect their children from schools at all sorts of time during the day. "Sorry picking my son up from school in ten minutes." Maybe their son is at nursery school, but even then, do nursery schools finish at 10.30 in the morning? Me thinks not.

"No, I'm alright thanks," or, "You're alright," are heard several times a day. Against the rules, but it does make you feel like saying, 'I wasn't asking about your health, and mine's fine, but thanks anyway.

Known to market researchers simply as dragged-ups, these are the people who just totally ignore you once you have spoken to them. Didn't their parents explain its just plain rude? It can be said that we, by approaching members of the public are intrusive. This should not be the case, if a market researcher is worth their salt. It is our job to obtain the general public's opinion on whatever subject. If you don't have an opinion or don't want to take part, that's fine. At the end of the day we are just doing a job. I have yet to meet anyone who has no opinions at all, from the price of a pint to who should win the next election. It's our right to say what we think. All we do is collect your answers, making the respondent feel at ease while doing so.

We are of course never supposed to be rude, but, we are after all, only human. I rarely lose my temper, well that's not true, what I should say is that I rarely lose my temper at work. I can scream at my family as I'm sure they can testify. However, I have on the odd occasion lost the plot while working. One such time was when I was working at a local shopping mall, I saw a gentleman, or so I thought, who would fit my quota, so asked in my sweetest of voice, "Excuse me Sir…"

"Fuck off. Get a proper job," was the reply I got, as he walked away.

"Excuse me. This is a proper job," I said, feeling the redness rushing to my cheeks. Then, without thinking it through, I added, "Why, if I didn't do this type of job I'd have missed the opportunity of talking to a moron like you." I couldn't believe I'd said it.

He turned and made a two finger gesture.

"Very mature," I shouted after him.

A lady standing close by smiled at me. "Good for you, love. Some people are so rude."

I smiled back, but felt very embarrassed, not only by the fact that I had been spoken to in such a fashion, but also that I had not kept my cool and had lowered myself to his level. But, as I said, we're only human.

In Peterborough for no particular reason, a lot of the members of the public assume we are catalogue ladies, selling membership to various club books, Littlewoods or Next. Sometime you don't even get the chance to explain that you're not selling anything. People assume that you're a club book lady. This once happened to Jenny, a colleague and good friend of mine. For some unexplained reason she snapped. It was funny to watch my usually calm friend losing the plot, if only for a moment.

A young women aged about thirty five, dressed in somewhat scruffy jeans and a t-shirt drizzled with food stains, her hair greasy from several weeks of neglect, walked up to Jenny while we were working as a team of five interviewers, from a venue.

"You a fucking club book then?" She almost spat the words in Jenny's direction.

Jenny, without changing her facial expression, replied, "Do I look like a fucking club book? Piss off."

Miss Scruffy eyed her up and down, then must have decided from Jenny's intense stare that it really wouldn't be worth pursuing her initial line of enquiry any further, in any shape or form. She turned and left.

We all hid our I.D. badges for about half an hour, just in case she reported us to someone!

For every ignorant person, there are hundreds of polite, nice people. Not everyone has the time in the day to complete a survey – understandably – but I have been thanked by many members of the public for asking them, even if they have declined to take part.

What would I use for my excuse if I had ever been approached? Guess I would go for the smile after trying not to make eye contact while turning a deep shade of purple.

Good We Have A Driver

Occasionally interviewers get the odd chat up line, or even asked out on a date. I guess this is because we are sat with a perfect stranger for twenty five minutes or more while interviewing, smiling as we do this, listening to their problems, providing a sympathetic ear. Everyone who agreed to complete a survey is offered a cup of coffee or tea. They are under no pressure, and overall, it's a pleasant way of spending half an hour with someone.

I have always called people "Darling" even when not working, but have found that this can be taken out of context on occasion, if only by a few. I once stopped a woman who gladly agreed to do a survey, but only if I promised not to call her "Darling," as she found it annoying. Fair enough, so what did I do as I sat her down in front of a laptop to complete the survey, "Take a seat, darling" I said, only to have to apologise very quickly once the words had escaped my lips.

We often conduct surveys on alcohol, and the largest part of these quotas have to be male.

I approached a middle aged man for one such survey. He had a mild smell of beer on his breath, but wasn't drunk.

"Excuse me, sir. We're conducting a survey on alcohol. Would you be willing to take part?"

"You're talking to the right man. Just had a pint," he smiled back

"You sound perfect, my darling," I answered showing him my ID card.

"You look a lot better in the flesh, Shelley," he grinned.

"Thank you, darling," I said still smiling, but now a little worried he'd noticed my name so quickly on the ID card. "It's just in this building here," I pointed.

"Let's do it then Shelley," he agreed.

Once I'd sat him down after making him a coffee I asked for his name address and telephone number, a necessity for every interview.

"Well you've got my telephone number now," he giggled.

"Yes." I smiled back.

Not heard that one before, I thought.

"What brands of beers can you think of? Please mention all those that come to mind."

"Now you're asking," he smiled. "Well there's Boddingtons, John Smiths, Carling…"

I looked up after entering all his reply's on the computer.

"You've got lovely eyes, Shelley," he grinned back at me.

"Thank you. And which brand do you drink most often?"

"No, I mean it. You've got lovely eyes." His stare was intense.

"Thanks," I said. "So which brands do you drink most often?"

"Well most of them really. Are you free tonight?"

"That's very lovely of you to ask, but I come with a husband, children, and even grandchildren," I joked.

"All the good ones are married," he sighed.

"So which brands would you say you drink most often?"

"Oh put down Boddingtons. Are you really married?"

"Boddingtons." I entered this information. We were now up to question three. "And yes, I'm really married. Which of these beers have you heard about?" I asked, showing him the computer screen loaded with pictures of every brand of beer you could imagine.

"Do you and your husband get on alright?" he asked.

"Yes," I smiled back. "So which of these beers have you heard of?"

"He's a lucky man. Oh, just put all of them down."

"All of them," I enquired, not looking up.

"So you wouldn't consider even coming for a drink?" He was persistent, I'd give him that.

"No it's lovely of you to ask, but as I said I'm married."

That should do it.

"What he doesn't know won't hurt him," he said.

Ignore him. Best policy.

"And which of these have you seen, heard, or read about recently?" I asked showing him yet another screen full of different types of beer.

"All of them. So you're a real married woman, Not many of you about." He was still grinning.

"Yes, really married. All of them you say?" Question four, we were making progress.

"Knew you'd be lovely the moment I saw you."

"Thanks. You said you'd seen this brand advertised. Can you tell me where it was you saw it advertised?"

"Don't know. Probably telly. So how long have you been married?"

"Telly." I tried to continue. "Again, you said you'd seen this brand advertised. Can you tell me where it was you saw the advert?" I asked, showing him the next screen.

"Aren't you going to tell me?" he asked.

"Long time," I answered. "And this brand?"

"All on the telly. I've got property. Nice house in the country."

"And this brand?" I asked, showing him the next page of the survey.

"All on telly. What harm can one drink do?"

"Darling, I'm very flattered, but I really can't go out with you."

"Knew you were lovely," he said yet again.

And so the interview went on. I asked a question, he asked me out. I caught sight of one of my colleagues interviewing a respondent next to me. They smiled. We'd heard this all before.

"And finally, sir, if we needed to get back to you about this survey would you be willing to be re contacted?"

"So you're going to phone me then?" he smirked.

"No, it wouldn't be me," I explained. "It would be someone from Head Office."

"Yeah, if that's what you want me to think." He grinned from ear to ear.

As I handed him his thank you note and pen he touched my hand.

"Be hearing from you then." Again, the smirk.

"Umm," was all I could manage.

"That was a 'D' for difficult one," my colleague laughed as we walked out into the sunshine.

"Yeah got to give him ten out of ten for persistency though."

One of the best chat up lines I have ever heard happened one day when I was working in Peterborough. It was a nice atmosphere working there that day. The leaves had just begun to drift off the trees in the avenue, making way for the new ones to appear the following spring. People seemed to be ambling along in no particular hurry.

The sun shone down. It was just one of those very pleasant autumn days.

I stood in the warm sunshine, looking for my next respondent to come along. Someone pattered me one the shoulder, as I turned, I saw this huge bear of a man smiling back. He was supporting a walking stick rather than it supporting him. His bright blue eyes looked down at me. His age I would have thought to be around eighty five-ish.

"My darling," he said with a slight Polish ascent, "I have been watching you from afar. I like for you very much. You come dancing with me. A few brandies, some candlelight. It will be lovely for us both."

My smile broadened. "That sounds wonderful," I truthfully admitted. I could almost picture the scene. "But I have a husband."

He thought for a slightest of moments, "Good we have a driver then." With that he gave a little chuckle, leaving me to maybe think about what a lovely evening I was going to miss out on. I could tell from the roguish twinkle in his eye that he was still a ladies man.

When I told Peter, he smiled. "Wonder how many times in the war he used that one."

Never Assume

On a not so warm day, I had begun to give up hope of ever recruiting someone, having stood outside for nearly an hour. No one would stop, though who could blame them as the weather was appalling, miserable, cold, and topped off with a steady flow of rain?

Finally, I approached a woman in her mid thirties. "Excuse me, madam, we're conducting some market research. Would you be willing to do a survey?" I asked, in my sweetest of voices.

"OK yar," she answered in a Afrikaans's drawl.

"Can I just ask, do you have a UK address?" I checked.

"Yar, have lived here for over a year," came the reply.

"You sound as if you come from my part of the world."

"You come from South Africa?" she asked.

"Well no. I was born in Zambia," I said, knowing my English accent was not giving away my origins. "But I've lived here a long time. Did you come over here for the sunshine?" I joked.

"What sunshine?" she asked, my humour obviously lost on her.

"I know. Not sure if you ever really get used to the weather."

Better not to make light of anything, I decided.

After checking that she was eligible to take part in the survey, I began to walk her toward the venue where the survey was to be completed, making small talk as we went.

"So you've lived here for a year? Do you like it?"

"Oh yar, it's so difficult at home, too much crime there, you know."

I nodded as if I did.

"I like it here, even though the weather is so cold," she carried on. "Brought my three little ones over. They have settled really well."

"Well that's a relief if the kids are happy," I started.

"Well they're very happy. But to tell the truth, I have concerns about my ten year old. She's going through a very difficult patch. Don't know if it's not depression. Her behaviour is getting out of hand."

"I'm sorry to hear that," I said.

"Yes, I can't say that she's truly happy here."

"Maybe she's missing her friends from home."

"Don't think it's that, but I never know what mood she'll be in by the time I get home."

"Have you taken her to a doctor?"

"No," her reply came back at me sharply.

Once in the venue, seating her in front of a laptop, I began to explain that it was a self completion survey, running through how it was a touch screen laptop. "Couldn't be easier," I reassured her.

Finally, I checked to see if she wanted a cup of coffee or tea, then, I left her to complete the survey on her own.

By the time I returned once again with the next respondent, she was nearing the end of the survey the computer had chosen for her. Cossett's had designed software to enable them to tell, after a few brief questions, which survey out of fifty or more, any respondent would fit into. All very innovative.

"Thanks ever so much," I looked across at her.

"Not a problem," came the reply with that unmistakable twang accent.

"Hope everything works out with your daughter," I smiled

"What daughter?" she queried.

I walked toward her, "Your daughter with the problems. Really hope it works out for her." My tone was hushed, aware that this was not something I should be mentioning out loud in a room full of strangers, all busy completing their own surveys.

She looked at me blankly.

"Your ten year old," I reminder her, not sure why it was necessary to remind her of the problems she had at home.

"Oh, Sofie? Maybe I'll take her to the vet's tomorrow," she replied

"Vets?" The bewilderment clearly showed on my face.

"Yar, the vet's." She smiled back as if nothing was wrong.

"You're taking you daughter to the vet's?" I stupidly questioned.

"No, my cat." She looked equally bewildered.

"I'm sorry. I thought you said your daughter."
"No Sofie's a cat."
Then the penny dropped.
"Well they're my family," she finalised.
"Yes," I agreed hoping that she couldn't see that I didn't make that connection at all. "Of course they are."
Lesson three hundred and twenty one: never assume!

Another incident with someone from my part of the world, involved a fellow colleague, Jenny. Jenny was aware of my origins, as were several of my other colleagues. Sometimes during a lunch break, I would be asked to say something in a Zambian accent. Although my accent is now sounding more and more like an English person impersonating someone from Zambia. I remember just a few of the phrases from my childhood, although Peter claims that whenever I lose my temper, the Yarpee in me comes out in full force. I can still swear in Afrikaner. Some things are just never forgotten.

Jenny has a similar sense of humour to myself, and we found most things funny. This would sometimes get us into difficulty trying to control ourselves from laughing out loud at the various situations that would arise when recruiting or interviewing the public. This occasion turned out to be one of those.

I was already interviewing a respondent when Jenny appeared at the door of the venue with her newest respondent.

Most venue based surveys have a sort of library feel to them, especially if the survey is completed by the respondent and not us as interviewers. It has a hushed silence about it. This was one of those types of surveys.

As Jenny entered the room, she asked her respondent, in a breathless voice, brought on by the six flights of stairs it had taken her to climb to get to the room where the surveys were being completed.

"And can I just ask you name?" Jenny said while seating her respondent at a computer.

"Mary Ying," answered the South African
"Mary Ying," Jenny repeated.
"No, Mary Ying," the South African retorted
"Mary Ying," Jenny smiled.
"No Mary Ying, Ying." This time said with a little more force.
"Mary Ying." Jenny said beginning to attempt to write down the name of her respondent.

"YING," came back an even louder reply.

"Yes YING," Jenny sounded back almost as loudly.

"No, No YING, as in nat old, YING." The South African almost spat back.

By this time we had all looked over. I caught Jenny's eye she was expecting me to understand what she obviously couldn't.

"Ying, Ying, as in nat old," Jenny repeated.

"Yes, Ying," said the South African, pleased that Jenny had now finally understood her.

"Mary Ying," Jenny said to reassure herself.

"No, YING AS IN NAT OLD," shouted the women.

At this point I decided to stroll over. It was time for my expertise.

"Sorry my darling," I began, "your name is Mary Ying."

"NO." bellowed the women in case people in the street below couldn't hear her. "YING YING AS IN NAT OLD."

I looked at Jenny and she looked at me.

"YING," she shouted in desperation.

"Ying," Jenny and I said now both sure we understood.

"YING, YING," she said grabbing Jenny's pen from her hand.

"Ying, Ying," she said as she wrote her surname on the recruitment sheet.

We all stared down at the sheet, all longing for this to be cleared up. To find out this poor woman's name was now the centre of our universe. Everything depended on us knowing the answer. Forget the unanswered questions of all time, it was imperative to our to harmony, to our ying and yang, that we knew her name.

"Ying, as in nat old," she said as pointed toward the recruitment sheet.

"Young, as in not old," Jenny said with relief, beyond words.

I just had to walk away at this point, biting down hard on my finger as I did so.

Once outside again Jenny came towards me holding both side of her body, tears flowing down her cheeks.

"You were loads of help," she laughed and snorted. "Thought you were from Africa."

"I am," I managed to get out between gulps of laughter.

"No, I think you're from Huddersfield," she giggled.

90 Mile Down The Road

Depending on the type of job you are given, you are always sent what we call a quota. This determines how many male or females we have to recruit, the ages of respondents needed, and the type of work they do – a white collar worker or blue collar worker.

A/B is for professionals such as doctors and lawyers, people who have hit the height of their profession. -C1 is anyone doing a white collar job or very skilled employment such as a nurse etc. - C2 are blue collar workers which are skilled, say a sheet metal worker or engineer. -D is a worker who can be trained to do their job within a couple of days, like a sales assistant. -E could be for someone who is out of work for more than six months, or on any sort of state benefit or only receiving a state pension.

There is a market researcher's bible to help us keep abreast of occupational coding. This book called the Occupational Grouping Guide, which as a market researcher you constantly have your nose in to check you have the correct coding.

Area and locations determine how easy or difficult it is to complete the quotas sent. We sometimes work in a small market town I shall name as Witchwood, so as to hide it's true identity. None of us like working there. It always seems to have a grey sky even on the brightest day. The population is tiny. There are loads of immigrant workers from Portugal, none of whom seem to speak English. When you approach these people you know what the reply will be.

"No speeky English." Unable to recruit them due to my own lack of Portuguese and their lack of English make's my chances of finding someone I need much slimmer.

This small market town has only one high street. There we stand, all four interviewers, in a space not big enough to seal an envelope, waiting for the next person to walk down the road, it can take half an hour before this happens, only to find that they are over ninety or not in the least interested in taking part in a survey, that's if they speak English. It's always a long day when we work there.

Drug deals are often taking place in the telephone box near to where we stand. Now I know how much a half bag of brown cost and what times the Bros will meet up to do the "deal". Why they all call each other Bros is something still unexplained to me, and why they all have to talk in such loud voices while doing these deals is a total bewilderment. I would have thought that to talk in hushed tones would have been more appropriate if you were dealing with a class "A" drug. Maybe the class "A" drugs they use and deal in makes you slightly deaf, it's a possibility.

There are no professional people living in this area, so any quota sent is total nonsense. We spend many an happy hour looking for ABC1's knowing that we could stand there until hell freezes over and they wouldn't be forthcoming.

The venue we use is the Old Court Rooms. The acoustics are just plain awful. If we are fortunate enough, to all recruit someone at the around the same time, and then all interviewing at the same time, be it at different tables, each interviewer cannot hear themselves ask their own questions, but rather the tail end of the question of whoever is sitting next to them or the answer of their respondent. This in turn prompts the respondent you are interviewing to be given an answer which technically is not theirs, an example of this would be.

"Which brand of beer have you seen or heard of?" I would ask.

"Carling," I would hear from the next table where another interview would be taking place.

"Oh yeah, there's Carling," your respondent would reply.

It makes nonsense of the whole thing.

I'm sure there are "normal folk" who live there, but they must shop somewhere else, maybe because it's safer!

You never know where you will be sent to work, some days it is local, sometimes we are sent to other parts of the country. I had heard about working in some of the venues close to London. How differently they worked, using the Essex "Hard Sell" to recruit, but I was unaware as to just how different it truly was from my part of the world, Norfolk.

The phone rang one evening.

"Hello Shelley." Julie's voice had sincere warmth about it. "Got a venue based job in Chelmsford next Friday. Could you go along there?"

"Yeah sound's fine," I said checking my dairy while trying to hold the phone to my ear.

"Oh thanks. Couldn't get anyone else to do it." Julie sounded relieved.

"Yeah that's fine," I said.

"Thanks I'll put you down for that one."

"Ok what's the venue address?"

Julie went on to explain how to get to Chelmsford, where to park, etc.

Friday arrived, and as I was driving the ninety miles to Chelmsford, Julie's words began turning over in my head. 'Couldn't get anyone else to do it...'

Don't be silly, I reassured myself. *It's not the other side of the world. It's ninety miles down the road.*

When I got there, I walked into the Pub Julie had said I'd be working in.

"Excuse me I'm here to do Market Research," I said to the pretty blonde girl behind the bar.

"Umm," she said staring straight through me. "They're upstairs."

I looked around.

What stairs?

"Upstairs?" I questioned.

The pretty blonde girl rolled her eyes. Obviously she was talking to a dumb Northerner from Norfolk. "Round the corner, there's the stairs," she said flatly.

"Thank you," I smiled back.

So I went upstairs and found the room, where there were two women sitting.

"Hello."

The women looked up and nodded.

"Alright if I make a coffee?" I asked.

"Help yourself," said the older women without looking up from the newspapers she was reading.

"My name's Shelley."

"I'm Doreen, this is Lilly," said the younger looking of the two. "Haven't seen you here before, dear."

I opened my mouth to reply but was cut short by Lilly.

"Where you from then?"

"Norwich," was all I managed to get out.

"Norwich. That's near the Broads, isn't it?" shouted Doreen, she must have thought I was hard of hearing. "You went there once didn't you, Lilly, for a holiday?" she said at the top of her lungs, maybe Lilly was the deaf one.

"Yes lovely there, lots of country side, and the food was lovely," Lilly bellowed back.

"Yes it's very nice on the," I tried joining in.

"Oh yes we really loved our week on the Broads, lots of peace and quiet." Lilly carried on. "Burt loved it, all those animals in fields."

I now decided the Lilly was trying to tell someone I couldn't see in the next room, as well as Doreen and myself about her hols in Norfolk. She seemed to get louder with each new bit of information.

"You said it was a bit expensive to hire the boat you stayed on?" screamed Doreen, sitting inches away from both of us.

"Yes bit expensive, but worth every penny though," Lilly howled back. "Go back again in a jiffie, we would."

"Hello you two, who's this?" I heard from the other side of the room, as a woman in her late fifties came through the door.

"This is… What was your name dear?" Lilly looked in my direction.

"Shelley, her name's Shelley," Doreen hollowed. "She's from the Broads."

"Well Norwich…" I tried to correct her.

"Yes that's right from Norwich dear," Doreen echoed back. "Lilly went on holiday there. Do you remember Natalie, Burt and her had a lovely time? She says there was lots of animals in the field."

"Course I remember. It was about three years ago, wasn't it Lilly?" Natalie screamed in reply.

They must all have hearing problems I thought as my ears began to ring.

"You said it was expensive to hire the boat thingie," shouted Natalie who was now standing next to the chair I had perched myself on.

"Yes. Bit expensive but well worth it," Lilly came back in a voice any Town Crier would have be grateful for.

And so the conversation went on for the next ten minutes. They repeatedly stated that The Broads had "lovely food, ever so cheap, lovely animals in the fields, but that it was a bit expensive to hire a boat thingie". By the end of the ten minutes I began to wonder if they thought I was maybe a bit thick coming from the North, that's why they had to tell me over and over again the same thing. "Lovely food, nice animals, boat hire expensive.' If I wasn't deaf when I'd entered the room, it was a sure bet I would leave it hard of hearing.

Thankfully, the supervisor who was to be running the venue arrived, introducing herself to me, but again with the volume turned up, I guessed for my benefit – the thicky from Norfolk.

"Hello I'm Martha, you must be Shelley. Head Office told me you was turning up today," Martha shouted inch away from my face. "Well girls, I'll brief you on today's job and then it's out we go." She turned, projecting her voice across the room.

"We was just saying, Shelley's from Norfolk, you know where Lilly went on holiday," Doreen screeched toward Martha.

"Oh yes, I know." Martha bellowed back.

Losing the will to live as Doreen ran through the whole lovely food, nice animals boat expensive thing again, the realisation dawned on me, that the high pitched volume of their voices was not just for my benefit, it was normal for to them.

Once outside I began to try recruiting

"Excuse me Madam," I began

"Yeah?"

"We're conducting Market Research…"

"Nar Nar thanks," was all I got.

And so the day went on. I have to say everyone stopped, smiled pleasantly at me, then again the same, "Nar thanks."

Lunch time was fast approaching. As yet I had only recruited two bodies. The first was a lad who was from Cumbria on holiday. The second was a young woman who was in Chelmsford to take part as a witness in a court case and had a couple of hours to kill before she would be called. I glanced over at Lilly.

"Hello luv, you drink beer, do you want to do a survey?" she asked a young man, before almost dragging him towards the venue. He didn't seem able to put up any resistance. It would have been futile anyway. Lilly had the magical touch.

Lilly's approach was against everything I'd been taught about recruiting. We aren't allowed to tell the members of the public what the survey was about, to ensure that they have an open mind before commencing the survey. No physical contact to be made with respondents, but Lilly had caught hold of her young man's arm and led him to the doorway, ensuring no escape could be made. Everything in her approach was incorrect, but it worked every time.

Lilly headed out into the Chelmsford sunshine, smiling broadly having sat her young man in front of the laptop leaving him to complete it on his own.

"How many have you done, Lilly?" I asked peering over her shoulder to read her recruitment sheet.

"He wos number ten," she bellowed back.

"I must be doing something wrong then. I've only done two."

"Well if you don't mind me saying, lovie, you just has to drag them in."

My expression must have said it all.

"I know it's not the way you've been shown, but you're in Chelmsford now. We have our own way of doing things." Lilly suppressed her tone, I imagine as close as Lilly could get to a whisper, which I think could be heard in Luton.

Groupies

Doing Market Research in any city you get to know the regulars. People working in local shops and individuals like Alice who visiting the town on a regular basis for bit of shopping. You find you are on a nodding acquaintance with Big Issue sellers, market stall holders happy to smile at you from a distance, but very unhappy if you stand in too close a vicinity to their stalls. Of course, as with any city or town, you see the sadder cases, like the heroin addicts who wander the streets daily. Their eyes tell the saddest of tales, lost in their own world, their clothing hanging off their wasted limbs. Even these unfortunate individuals give you a smile as they pass you by, knowing that they know you from somewhere, but unaware that they saw you the day before standing in the same place.

Then there are our groupies, similar to Alice in so far as they want to do a survey, but dissimilar in that doing a survey is more of an addiction for them. The groupies or regular respondents come in all sorts of shapes and sizes, age groups and gender. They will approach you in the street to check what the survey is about. Some will even lie about their profession or age just to get to do a survey. They understand as much as we do about market research, knowing that we will have a quota to achieve. In truth, we should not interview these regulars. The rules in the Market Research Code of Practice state that you should only interview the same person once every six months, however, some of them are hard to say no to. Once in the venue they revel in being made a bit of a fuss of, ordering tea or coffee, taking their time to complete the survey, relishing each question. I'm not saying these people are peculiar. Whatever gets you through the day, I say. Our surveys give them a bit of company, in nice surroundings. One of our groupies from Norwich once told me that it was well worth the £2.80 bus fare each day to travel in to Norwich, to help us out by doing a survey. She explained it would cost more to have a coffee in Costa's, so I guess the bus fare was worth it. In some cases, we are possibly the only people they speak to all day.

One character we all know in Norwich is Ned. Ned is a large chubby man, whose ruddy cheeks tend to hang either side of his face, giving him the features of a British Bull Dog. Ned has a vacant expression with eyes that stare out into the beyond. Summer or winter Ned supports a large woolly hat perched rather than placed on top of his head. It resembles an ill-fitting tea cosy. He always wears a Norwich City Supporters tee shirt which during the winter months is worn on top of his winter overcoat. Ned's one true love is his ancient Sony radio, which he holds delicately, with those oversized hands almost engulfing it from view, in front of his bulky frame.

Ned's vocation and life purpose is to pace round the city of Norwich while listening to the radio. Ned is on incapacity benefit. We have been told he was once, "someone" in the city, high up in corporate banking. The story goes that he then suffered a severe breakdown. He is always happy to smile at you, but the saying, "The lights are on but no one's at home" springs to mind each time I meet him. Ned seems content with his lot. I hope he is for his sake, but it still saddens me when I catch sight of him.

I had been booked to work at our normal venue in Norwich. It was nice working close to home, but sometimes you can meet so many people you know, it makes recruiting difficult, as you have to stop to have a chat.

It was a bright day. I stepped out of the mall entrance were I had parked my car and looked up at the tiny clouds bouncing around in the sky. It was going to be a good day. People were more likely to stop on such a day. Arriving at the room of the venue, after climbing the six flights of stairs, I managed a breathless hello to everyone there, then helped myself to a coffee.

Seconds after I had sat down, a new interviewer I hadn't met before entered the room, breathless and perspiring somewhat. He looked about thirty six, very thin, dressed in a suit that I would have guessed was bought for him some time ago as the sleeves and trouser bottoms were just that tad too short. It looked as if it had been bought by his mum for a family wedding when he was a teenager.

"Those stairs are something else. We're thinking of buying a flag and sticking it in the ground here, to show where the summit is." I pointed to the ground in front of me.

"Yeah," he let his breath go.

"Hi, I'm Shelley. This is…" I went on to introduce the others: Sarah, Simon, Ruth and Jonathan.

"I'm Steve. Never worked in Norwich before. I'm from Cambridge," he said, now almost in complete control of his breathing.

We all fussed round the new boy, making him welcome, all moaning relentlessly about the stairs at the venue. I think Steve got offered at least three cups of coffee from all of us. After a short briefing on the job for the day, it was time to face our public.

Steve obviously, keen to complete the quota for that day, was first out into the streets.

"That Steve's a bit keen," said one of my fellow colleagues.

"Yeah, he'll learn," I smiled back.

After an hour, poor Steve had yet to recruit his first respondent.

"I don't understand it," Steve confided in me. "Is it always this difficult in Norwich to get someone in?"

"No, maybe your just having a bad day." I hoped I sounded sympathetic. "We all have them."

"I don't," resounded Steve. "I'm the best recruiter in Cambridge."

"Not to worry," but thought him a bit of a big-headed.

Another hour or so went by and Steve was still standing alone, no one happy to stop for him.

"Don't think much of this place." Steve snorted, obviously fed up with what was turning out to be a "Norway" which in Market Research terms means "Zero Point", meaning you haven't managed to recruit anyone. Norway's origins are from the Eurovision Song Contest from a few years ago, when they scored zero.

I like to think that I'm not a territorial person, after all I am a child of the sixties – all that Love and Peace. I've always agreed with the lyrics of that song, *Melting Pot*. "What we need is a great big melting pot," but Steve was now criticising the place that I lived. People here were nice, pleasant to talk to. If they didn't have time to do a survey so what? They always declined in a polite way, well most of the time.

"What don't you like about it Steve?" I asked, a bit more sharply than I'd intended.

"No one stops for you. They're rude," he began.

"I find everyone here very polite," I cut in curtly.

Steve realising he'd hit a roar nerve, backed down. "I'll just go over here." He nodded to the other side of the street.

It was not until late afternoon that Steve appeared in the doorway of the venue.

"Take a seat here Sir," Steve said pointing to a chair. "Would you like tea, coffee?"

The three interviewers in the room all looked up.

"Christ he's brought in Ned," whispered Sarah.

Ned stared about the room still clutching his Sony radio which had now been turned off, woolly hat perched on top of his large head, cheeks hanging south wards.

"Tea –coffee ?" Steve questioned again.

"Can Ned read?" I hissed at Sarah.

Sarah raised her eyes to the heavens. "Didn't know he could speak..." she mumbled back.

"Tea, five sugars," Ned's gruff voice spoke out.

"Tea, five sugars," Steve shouted, to Simon across the room.

Simon frowned, it wasn't really his job to make refreshments for Steve's respondent, but as he was stood close to the kettle he did as he was told.

"Now this is extremely easy," Steve went on.

"I know." Ned said blankly, as if he did this all the time.

"It's all touch screen," Steve said placing the pen onto the screen. "Shall I put your radio on the table here?" Steve reached out to take the radio from Ned's grasp.

"No," Ned shouted clutching his dear beloved radio into his broad chest.

Steve, unfazed by this minor detail, carried on. "These are the questions I asked you outside. You're fifty seven years old and live in the Anglia region..."

Ned's glaze turned to the bright lights of the laptop screen, his radio tucked under his left arm, protected and safe from harm.

"Yeah," he agreed as Steve continued putting in the small amount of information he received from Ned outside.

"There. That's all there is to it, I'm going to leave you to complete the survey by yourself. If you've got any questions just ask Simon over there and he'll be happy to help you." With that Steve collected his clip board and was gone.

Simon was now standing by my side. "He's been in before," Simon whispered.

"Who Ned?"

"Yeah. Comes in every six months. Thinks it's his assessment."

"Assessment?" I looked puzzled.

"Yeah, Ned had a break down some years ago. He used to be something big in the city. Comes in here every six months, has a cuppa, does the survey, and leaves it till six months to the day before he comes in again."

I was now having to lip read Simon's words, as they were so hushed.

I looked over in Ned's direction. His hand delicately touched the screen with the pen issued to him by Steve, happily reading the questions before him, a small smile crossing his face as he did so. A sparkle in his eyes, he looked alive, something I had never seem happen on that well worn face.

"Didn't know you'd be doing your bit for society when you started doing this," Simon smiled.

The blankness of my expression showed I didn't understand what Simon meant.

"Makes Ned feel important, doing the survey. Look how much he's enjoying himself."

I glanced over in Ned's direction and see a grin taking up his entire face. He was in the full throws of the survey, enjoying being worthy, being asked his opinion. Maybe he thought of it as an assessment, but it was the happiest I ever seen him. It brought a lump to my throat. I left the room before anyone could see me blubber.

I was standing next to Steve when Ned appeared as if from nowhere, some three quarters of an hour after first entering the venue.

"Tar mate," Ned grunted, face now back to it normal blankness, "Be back in six months."

The Sony radio held tightly to his chest, Ned turned and left to complete his route around the city.

"Another satisfied customer," Steve grinned.

"Yeah," I agreed leaving Steve unaware of how he had made Ned feel like a human being if only for short time.

Not long after Ned's assessment, Simon confided a tale of an interview he had completed at a local council estate which had the reputation of being, shall we say rough round the edges.

He had been working a pack of work door to door. This meant knocking on doors and trying to get someone to complete a survey if they fitted the quota.

Simon knocked at a particularly run down house, mattress in the garden, combined with enough rubbish to fill a wheelie bin. He knew it was going to be one of those houses where you declined to take a seat, but he need to find someone on state benefit to complete the quota. This area was renowned for people being out of work. Finally a man answered the door and agreed to do the survey.

Toward the end of the survey the man looked directly at Simon and asked, "How long will it be before I hear?"

Simon, taken back by this question, replied, "Before you hear what?"

"Yeah how long?"

"I'm sorry, sir…"

"How long before I know?" the man asked again, politely.

"Before you know?" Simon confessed to sounding confused at this point.

"If I got the job," the man said plainly.

Simon twigged. The chap thought he was applying for a job throughout the questionnaire. Had not realised it was a survey.

"At least he was looking for work," Simon grinned.

Market Researchers Don't Count

One of my favourite types of surveys are, kid's surveys. Children love to be asked their opinion. They know everything there is to know about current adverts that you might be asking them about and never decline doing a survey. Some, depending on their age, might be a little shy when first answering questions, but most are full of ideas about the products or the advertising you are researching.

All kid's surveys must be conducted with a parent or guardian in attendance. There are, of course, very strict rules to interviewing a minor, all interviewers having to have had a CRB, police check to ensure that they are suitable to interview children.

On a lovely bright spring morning I was working in the Ipswich area, looking for children between seven and thirteen years old to interview. As I walked round a large council estate, I saw some children sitting on a garden wall.

"Hello." I greeted them.

"Yeah, wot you want?" grunted the oldest child aged about ten.

"I'm doing some market research, do you want to take part in a survey?" I smiled back.

"What's that then?" asked a petit girl sitting to the right hand side of the ten year old, who's attitude who would one day I'm sure turn him into Victor Meldrew.

"Well, I ask you a few questions about different things to do with adverts on telly, then you tell me what you think."

"OK then," she smiled back, as she jumped off the garden wall, "I'll do it."

"Is your mum or dad at home?" I enquired. "Because I have to ask them permission for you to do the survey."

"Mum's at home." She pointed to a house across the road.

"Well let's check she says it's alright." I said as I followed her across the road, "What's your name, love?"

"Kylie."

Kylie threw back the door with the force of someone three times her size, causing it to thud against the wall. I could hear her charging up the stairs to find her mum. As I stood waiting for Kylie and her mum to appear at the back door, several other children gathered by the gate.

"What's Kylie doing?" one of them asked me

"A survey," I answered

"What's a survey?" asked another small child.

"Oh, I'm just going to ask Kylie some question about cheesy dips, see what she thinks."

"I know about cheesy dips," shouted a small boy standing at the back of the crowd of youngsters, throwing his arm into the air as if he were in the school class room, begging to answer the questions.

"Do you? Would you like to do a survey after Kylie?" I asked, knowing what the answer would be.

"Yeah," came back the enthusiastic reply.

"Can I do one too?" shouted another little boy.

"And me," said another.

I had to smile.

If only all respondents were as happy to take part in a survey, this job would a walk in the park.

"Yes. I'll come and see you after Kylie's finished her survey."

"Hello." I heard a voice behind me.

"Hello Kylie's Mum," I smiled back, hoping I had guessed correctly as the young woman standing in the doorway could easily have been Kylie's older sister.

"Kylie says you want to interview her," the pretty young woman enquired.

"Yes we're doing some market research in the area with children, would that be alright?"

"Can't see why not. Kylie!" she shouted back into the house unnecessarily as Kylie was standing at her side, eager to take part.

I explained what was involved, gave Kylie's mum the relevant paperwork, and showed my ID card.

"Can I come in?" I asked.

"Shall we sit in the garden?" Kylie's Mum pointed to a small table and chairs on the patio.

Sitting down, I noticed the small group of children who had been keen to know what a survey was and now wanted to do one, had gathered at the gate, and gradually were edging their way into Kylie's garden.

"Right you lot," Kylie's Mum shouted, "Over there till we're finished." She pointed to a small lawn area.

"Well, Kylie, I'm going to ask you some question about an advert," I began.

Kylie's relished each question. She knew everything there was to know about the latest cheesy dips. It was a pleasure interviewing such a sweet little girl. The other kids had taken to playing football on the lawn. Now and then Kylie's Mum would scream at them to keep the noise down, her voice resembling a fish wife.

The interview nearly at an end, I began the closing questions.

"Well Kylie," I started, and then felt the thump as a football bounced off the side of my head.

"Bloody well watch what you're doing," came the fish wive's voice out of that tiny young mum's mouth. "You might bleedin' hit me next time."

I looked up to see the small group of kid scatter at her words, disappearing out of the garden gate with great haste.

My head was reeling, but I had to smile at Kylie's Mum's concerns that it would hit her next time.

Market researchers don't count, I guessed.

Suffer Little Children To Come To Me

There are of course some sad situations when doing any survey, and when it involves children, it's the worst. On another occasion when I was conducting a kiddie's survey I had a small entourage of small kids following me around a local housing estate where I was working, all asking what a survey was, then asking if they could do one to get the sparkly pen I would give them at the end of it. Unfortunately none of them were the right age to take part.

"Maybe next time when I come to do a survey, you can do it." I tried to explain, but of course they didn't understand, thinking that if they stayed with me long enough I would give in and include them.

"Go on misses, we'll do your survey," a small boy asked for the umpteenth time.

I smiled back at them. "Do you know any kids living round here aged seven?"

"Well the O'Reilly family live over there," grunted one small chap, "But I wouldn't go there."

"That bungalow?" I pointed in the direction he was looking.

"No 7," he pointed to a bungalow, "but they won't be allowed to do it."

"Well I can ask," I said walking towards No 7.

As I did so, the kids who had followed me for most of the morning, turned to leave.

"Bye," I shouted after them, but no reply came from any of them.

I should have known something was wrong then. Children even though you have told them they can't take part in the survey, still tend to stick around hoping to be included, or at the least watch as some other lucky child gets to answer the question. They look on in envy as you present that child with a sparkly pen for taking part in the survey, this small token of appreciation seeming to be on a par with the crown jewels.

As I approached I found the scruffy bungalow with windows smashed with a spider-web pattern that looked as if it had been caused by someone's head hitting it hard. Chipboard covered half the door instead of a glass panel. The un-kept garden was littered with crisp packets. There was a plastic wash basket which had been trampled on so that its side were buried into the mud of what was once a garden boarder. Two broken bicycles lay across the small path leading to the front door. Then the sight I'd seen many times before: a stained mattress thrown into the front garden, now soaked in rain from the many months it had laid there.

There was no door bell insight. Just two splintered wires hanging were once there'd been one. The door frame's paint was peeling, looking as if it would fall apart if I touched it. I decided to knock on the chipboard panelling.

The door opened abruptly. "Yeah what you want," asked a woman complete with a fag hanging out of her mouth.

"Morning. I'm doing some market research in the area. We're conducting surveys with children. I understand you have a little boy aged around seven years old. I was wondering if he would like to do a survey."

"What's in it for us?" she asked aggressively.

"Well the children get a pen," my answer was weak.

"Can I do it, Mum?" asked the small boy standing next to her, "Please, Mum can I?"

I smiled back at the lad. He was small even for seven, if he was seven. His hair cropped close to his scalp, food stains covering his faded tee shirt, his two front teeth missing, but the cheekiest grin.

"Please, Mum, can I?" He persisted.

"Will it take long?" she asked.

"About twenty minutes," I answered

"Please, Mum."

"Well as long as it don't take any longer, I've got lots to get on with," she said opening the door just wide enough for me to squeeze through.

Inside the house was worst than I had expected. I picked my way through the hallway littered with dirty washing, shoes, and cardboard boxes, piled high in ever available space. The smell hitting my nostrils was repulsive not only in the hallway, but as we walked passed two other rooms to get to the sitting room. It was apparent the smell was throughout the whole house.

Once inside the living room my eyes struggled to see anything. The room was filled with smoke. It filled every corner. The closed curtains hung from bits of string threaded through the plastic runner which was stained brown from the cigarette smoke.

Two sofas sat across from each other. On one sat a man in his mid thirty's his head only just visible from the cigarette smoke that engulfed him.

"What's she doing here?" he growled.

"Carl's doing a survey," she grunted back.

"Can we do one too?" I could hear some small voice, but it took me several minutes to focus where it had come from.

Two small boys sat at a chipped Formica table besides the sofa the man was sitting on, both with the inevitable number one cropped hair cuts. From what I could make out neither had changed their clothing for several days, let alone had any sort of bath.

"Shut up," the man shouted, dragging on the roll up.

I settled myself on the opposite sofa, trying to avoid what looked like several damp patches.

"Well, Carl, I'm going to ask you a few questions about cheesy dips and an advert you may have seem on TV."

Carl's grinned showing off those dimpled cheeks.

"What cheesy snacks can you think of?" I asked.

Carl went on to mention almost every brand I had on my list. His two brothers now joined us on the sofa, taking great interest in Carl's exciting adventure.

With every question I asked, Carl came back with a full explanation, telling me about the advert. Why he thought it was funny, lisping his words through the gap were his teeth would soon appear. His younger brothers added bits of information, also relishing doing their bit to helping their older brother.

Carl's Mother disappeared for a few minutes, returning with a tray with two plates each piled high with a full English fry-up. I saw the three boys look over, then drop their eyes towards the floor.

"Here." She shoved a plate toward the man, and then sat down with her plate on her lap. I watched as they both tucked into the soggy eggs, bacon, fried mushrooms, fried bread, baked beans, and a cup of steaming tea. They both managed to drop some of the runny egg down their tops as they ate.

Watching them was beginning to make me feel sick, but for some unknow reason it was compulsive viewing. Then the realisation struck. The three little boys clearly had not been fed that morning. I felt sure that even if they would be fed later, it certainly wouldn't be bacon and eggs. All three were underweight to the point of looking fragile even for their young ages.

I smile down at Carl. "Have you seen this advert before Carl?" I showed him a picture of the cheesy dip ad.

"Yeah, it's that one with…" Carl began.

"How the fuck is he supposed to know about that?" glared the man as he lit yet another roll up, having finished his meal.

"Children are really good at remembering adverts." I tried to keep the anger out of my voice.

"Fucking stupid if you ask me."

"I know this one Dad…" Carl began.

"Don't you answer me back, you stupid fuck-head," Carl's Dad screamed back.

Carl bowed his head.

"Is it OK if we carry on?" I asked, this time not managing to keep the fury out of my voice.

"Do wot yer fucking like," Carl's Dad shrugged.

Carl continue to know all there was to know about cheesy dips and snacks, but with every answer he would now glance over to check his dad glare wasn't on him. At the end of the survey I thanked Carl giving him and his two brothers some sparkly pens. The looks on their faces made me want to take them away from the awful smelly house, give them the biggest fry-up the world has ever seen, drive them straight down to Toys R Us and spend my life saving on them. Instead, I stood up, glad to be leaving that stinky room, that hell hole not fit for human beings. Certainly not fit those bright little boys, with their endearing grins.

I thanked the boys again but was unable to mutter anything to those parents. No, they weren't parents. There are no words to describe them.

"Thanks Misses," shouted Carl as I walked down the garden path.

"That's OK, Carl, thank you," I shouted back.

"Shut that fucking door and get back in here," I heard Carl's Dad bellow.

Walking away from that horrible, horrible place where three small boys lived in absolute squalor, I resolved to call the authorities as soon as I got home. It was 2005 for God's sake. What I had just witnessed could have been a scene from any Dickens novel. No one should have to live like that. Carl was such a bright little boy, living in fear of that grotesque couple with his two younger brothers.

I couldn't complete any further surveys. Carl's cheeky face popped into my head with each step I took towards my car.

I phoned Peter as soon as I got home.

"Christ Peter, it was awful. You should have seen those poor little kids."

"If you think you should phone someone, Shelley, that's what you should do," Peter agreed with me.

I checked the Yellow Pages for Social Services' telephone number. Waiting for the receiver to be picked up at the other end, I felt myself begin to shake with anger. It took over twenty minutes to finally get to speak to someone who seemed remotely interested in what I was saying.

"Oh yes the O'Reilly's at Drake View Close," came back a flat uninterested voice. "We're aware of the situation there. They have their own Social Worker allocated to their case."

"But I think those children are being physically abused, and most certainly mentally," I spluttered, tear's of frustration now falling down my face.

"As I said, we are aware of the situation Mrs Harris, but it was good of you to phone in."

"If you're aware, why isn't anyone doing something," I shouted down the phone.

"I know it's upsetting, but everything that can be done is being done," came back a slight softer tone. "We have to follow the guidelines…"

The conversation went on for ten minutes longer, with the same reply coming back at me although differently worded. By the time I had put down the receiver I felt drained.

Peter was, as always, wonderful when he came home that evening. Holding me close after I had ranted for half an hour about how useless the Social Services had been, and what a dreadful couple the parents were. Finally, I admitted just how desolate I felt leaving those little boys there, sobbing my heart out while Peter held me close without saying a word.

I phoned the help line for Cossett's the next morning asking to be taken off children's surveys for the next few months.

"Why is that Shelley?" asked the call operator.

"Oh, just would prefer to do venues for a bit," I lied.

"OK I'll take it off your profile," she said in a kind voice. Maybe she knew why I was requesting to be taken off this type of work, or maybe the upset still remained in my voice.

Even now I sometimes stop to think of Carl and his brothers. It still fills me with heartache thinking of them in that place. Do I do children's surveys now? Yes. Most children have happy lives. They make me smile with their answers to any questions put to them, seeing things that we as adult miss. Sparkly pen is still a great success. Kids just love to show them off to their friends. I wonder if Carl and his brothers still have those sparkly pens I handed them. I wonder if they are still living in that terrible environment, if their clothes are still dirty and soiled, knowing that they are not being fed and loved the way children should be. Most of all I wonder if I will ever be able to forgive myself for not being able to do more.

I Can't Read This

With some venue contracts we have to "pull in" as many as fifty six people in one day. So many women, so many men, different ages, and, of course, occupations. These contracts are achievable, but takes some doing. I don't think that some of the public we interview are always the quality of respondents our clients were asking for, but as an interviewer, you sometimes get bums on seat rather than quality bums on seats. Our instructions due to The Code of Practice are not to interview people we have interviewed in the past six months and not to interview groupies but with this number of respondents to achieve that is not always the case. Towards the end of the day if numbers are low, all rules go out of the window and we will get anyone we can.

One of my colleagues, John, is a sweet gentle soul, however it has to be said John, has no social graces to the point of being socially inept. Although an extremely clever man, I believe that he may be a sufferer of Asperger's Syndrome. Any conversation with John is totally one sided, John's reply's consisting of a simple yes or no. I have often wondered how he copes with this type of employment, but he manages to recruit his fair share of any quota set, working hard at his apparent disability.

I have watched him standing in the street, with a grin that goes ear to ear, wondering what on earth can be going through his head, his body stooped over with his I.D. card held out towards the oncoming public. He puts you in mind of a gun dog standing ready until such time as he can retrieve his prey.

John will recruit anyone as long as they can walk, talk and breathe. It's not so much as he doesn't think about the quota we have to fill, more I think that he possible doesn't truly see the individual he is approaching. Given his social graces John never indulges in light banter as he recruits. He will walk a couple of paces in front of people, without any discussion at all. None of your "Are you out shopping today," or, "Nice weather for the time of year."

Most venues are up several flights of stairs, which makes it awkward to recruit anyone with the slightest of disabilities. But I have seen John stop folk in wheelchairs, go through the total recruitment questionnaire before realising that they will be unable to make it up the stairs to the room where the venue is.

I didn't witness this particular incident as I was taking my own respondent into the venue. I promise that it's not that I am laughing at anyone with any disability, more should I say laughing at the situation that came about because of it.

John had been standing in his usual spot, when some poor chap fell over in front of him. Helped up by John, the chap thanked him for his kindness and a conversation ensued. One thing lead to another and John began recruiting him, checking through the recruitment questionnaire to check he was eligible to take part in the survey. To the amazement of other interviewers standing in close proximity to John, this chap was then lead towards the venue to take part in the survey. The question could have been asked, why didn't anybody stop the situation from worsening?

I was making a cuppa for the woman I had recruited when John entered the room followed by this chap, both breathing slightly heavily from the six flights they had just climbed. John sat his respondent down in front of the laptop, asking him to read the front page which begins every survey. John went over to the quota sheet on the table near the entrance, putting the details of his respondent down.

A small voice rang out across the room. "I'm afraid I can read this," the man politely said.

This is something that is sadly all too common place. Many people we recruit have reading or writing difficulties and are unable to complete these types of self completion survey.

Seeing that John was still deeply engrossed with entering the details on the quota sheet, I walked over.

"Can I help you darling?" I asked.

"I can't read this," he said again.

"Is the screen a bit dark?" I said not looking at him but trying to adjust the screen's brightness, hoping that that might be the problem, and not that he couldn't read.

"No, I can't read this," he said.

I looked up from the screen. His eyes were pale. Then I noticed the white stick. He was blind. No wonder he couldn't read a word of this.

How the hell did he make it up all those stairs?

My mind raced. How could I get around this one without upsetting this guy?

"I'm blind." He smiled.

"Oh my darling, I'm so sorry."

"One of those things," said this wonderful person.

"John." I called over. "This gentleman is unable to see the screen."

John looked up from the quota sheet, still oblivious to the problem.

"John." I said a bit more sternly. "This man can't do the survey."

John wandered over looking somewhat bewildered as to what I was talking about.

"John this gentleman can't do the survey. He has an eyesight problem." I stared back at John's uncertain expression.

"I can't see," the man interjected.

Still a blank expression from John.

There was no way round it, no way to fluff up the words. "This gentleman is blind, John," I said flatly.

Still no reaction from John, "John, this gentleman is blind." I spoke again.

"Oh," was all John managed.

"I'm so sorry my love." I turned towards the chap sitting patiently waiting for John to understand what was going on. "John, if you could help the gentleman downstairs."

"Thanks," said the chap standing up.

"John will help you downstairs," my voice sounded light but I was now nodding my head ferociously at John to indicate that this chap needed help.

After what seemed like a fortnight the penny fell, or should I say clanged like a church bell. John, still with a blank expression, took a pace toward this chap.

"Thank you for being so kind," the chap said.

"No thank you," I smiled as I left them to go back to making my own respondent a cup of coffee.

Moments had passed when I heard the chair fall over. Turning to see what was happening, I just couldn't believe what met my glance.

John was nowhere to been seen and the blind chap was hanging over a up turned chair, stumbling to regain his upright position.

"Oh my God, as you alright?" I ran over to help him.

"Yes, I'm OK," he said. "Always walking into something."

"Let me help you." I was now pulling this poor chap to his feet.

"Walked into a skip last week," he smiled, looking past me.

"I'm so sorry. Let's get you downstairs."

Another college who was supposed to be looking after the room, was standing near the doorway biting down hard on her own knuckle. I realised she was doing her best not to laugh out loud. I looked at her, furious that she should find this poor chap's disability such a laughing matter. My scowl must have said it all, but she made no attempt to change her attitude, biting down harder on her whole hand as I passed her, leading the blind man to the stair well and down the stairs.

It took some time to reach the front door.

As I opened the door I apologised for about the hundredth time, checking that he would be OK to carry on from there.

"I'll be fine," he assured me, walking away tapping the pavement with his stick as he went.

John was now standing in his normal spot, slightly bent over, ID card in hand ready for the next victim.

"For Christ's sake, John, that man was blind. What were you thinking about? You were supposed to help him down the stairs."

"He didn't say he was blind," John said blankly.

I looked at John, there was no point. He hadn't done anything wrong in his mind. He had recruited someone towards the quota. I just had to walk off. I decided to have a break, make myself a coffee. Back in the venue Katie, my college who had found the whole situation so amusing, walked over still trying to stifle the giggles.

"I'm sorry Shelley," she snorted. "It was when he fell over the chair."

"You're not nice," I stated

58

"I know, it was just…" She tried to begin but couldn't complete now she was laughing out loud.

"That poor man could have hurt himself." I sounded self righteous. "How he got up here in the first place I don't know."

"It was just well, John, he didn't notice." She was now holding her stomach "Then when that man was trying to feel his way round the room to find the door and fell over the chair." She was helpless with laughter now.

I did my best to keep a straight face. How had John not noticed? He had helped the man up when he had fallen in the street, then went on to recruit him. I imagined him leading the way up all those stairs to the venue, still not noticing this man's apparent blindness, that's if he spoke to him on the long climb to the room. I wondered if John's man had mentioned the fact that he was blind at any time, and if it would have made a difference. I doubted it. John was only doing his job, putting bums on seats.

Toughened Glass

As with all things, some days go so well you just can't believe it. We do occasionally have early finishes, being able to find all the correct type of respondents one after the other. One sunny summer's day, when the sky was the clearest blue, with not a hint of a shower, let alone the rain that had been forecasted last night on the box. I was completing a pack of work in Ipswich, having driven the sixty-four miles from Norwich earlier that day. After only four hours walking door to door I had found just about everyone I needed for my quota. Just two more interviews to complete then I'd be done. I was looking for young males aged eighteen to twenty four, what we called a C2 (blue collar worker.)

After completing my penultimate interview, I went back to my car to collect the last surveys and paperwork. I shut the car door with a bang and continued my stroll around the council estate. Feeling the sunshine on my back, I thought about how much I liked my job at that moment.

Strolling down the road I could see a young man of Caribbean decent sitting on the front step of his house enjoying the warmth of the day, Reggae music surrounding him from the ancient ghetto blaster which sat next to him on the step.

"Hello," I smiled broadly at him. "My name's Shelley. I'm doing some market research in the area. Would you help with a survey?"

"Yeah man, no probs," he smiled back showing the brightest, whitest teeth I have ever seen.

"OK. If I sit here next to you on the step?" I asked, already plonking my bum next to him.

"Yeah man no probs."

"As I said, my name's Shelley."

"Jo," he said, holding his hand out for me to shake.

"Hello, Jo," I said, taking his hand which engulfed mine.

"Beautiful day, ain't it," he smiled.

"Yeah, lovely."

"So wass this all about?" Jo enquired in his Caribbean drawl.

"Well I need to ask you some questions, just get your opinion on an advert," I answered as I prepared my paperwork.

"Ask away lady." Jo grinned back.

I liked Jo. Guess I envied his laid back approach to life. It was a spectacular day to just be sitting on your doorstep, watching the world go by. Jo fitted my quota exactly. He was a factory operative, the new politically correct title for someone who worked on the factory floor. He was twenty two years old, had lived in the UK for a year, but missed his family back home, missed his mum's cooking, he informed me.

Half way through the survey, Jo looked down at me. "You want some coffee Mrs Shelley, or maybe a cool drink?"

"Yeah thanks, Jo, that would be lovely, a cool drink."

"Back in a moment." Jo disappeared into the house.

"There you is Mrs Shelley." Jo held out a glass of fresh lemonade.

I continued the survey while sipping my drink of fresh lemonade. "This is really lovely," I said truthfully to Jo.

"Made it myself fresh this morning." Jo admitted.

We continued with the survey, although with Jo's laid back attitude it took a bit more time than usual to complete. Jo was such a pleasant young man, and he felt quite happy to take his time answering any questions put to him. No need to hurry on such a fine day, plus I struggled somewhat with his Caribbean accent. But Jo was more than patient with me.

"Well that's it, Jo, thanks ever so much, and thanks for the drink." I said putting my hand out to shake Jo's.

"No problems lady, you take care now," Jo's bright smile beamed.

I walked back to my car and fumbled in my jacket pocket for the keys. They weren't in there, so tried my handbag, balancing on one leg, clip board and finished questionnaire tucked under my other arm. Then I gave a sideways glance through my driver's window. There they were my keys, hanging from the ignition switch, dangling there without a care in the world. They didn't care if I got back in the car or not. They were in the place they were designed to be.

"No I don't believe it," I said out loud.

I fumbled some more in my handbag, realising I'd have to phone Peter. He'd have to drive all the way to Ipswich, bring his set of spare keys to rescue me. It wasn't going to be the quick trip home I'd planned, just one of those things.

I spent five more minutes of sifting through the rubbish in my hand bag. Only another woman would understand how important these things are: make-up bag, a copy of a phone bill I'd paid over three months ago, photos of the kids when they were at those loveable ages, all smiles with gaps in their teeth (*must update these now they're twenty-plus*), packet of empty headache tablets, (*must buy a new packet next time I pop in Boots*), five pens, only one of which worked, note pad with things scribbled on it when I was in a rush, that all important list of last Christmas's last minute presents – it was only seven months ago after all! There was all this stuff, but no phone.

Where is my bloody *phone?*

More fumbling then the slow realisation glimmered in my brain. I'd locked the sodden thing in the glove compartment before slamming the car door shut. There is nothing more annoying to not only yourself as an interviewer, but also your respondent if a mobile goes off mid interview. So clever me had left it in the car. I was just too thoughtful sometimes. What was I going to do now?

Phone box, I thought. *That's right Shelley, when in a corner think on your feet.*

After marching up and down several streets in the area near to Jo's house, the only phone box I found was out of action. Someone with a grudge against public phone booths, most probably because they're all painted red, had thought it a good idea to cut the connecting wire from the receiver to the phone apparatus.

" Bloody vandals," I heard myself hiss.

I had now been farting around for half an hour, wandering back to the car I knew what had to be done. Knocking on the door I could see no wrong in what I was about to suggest.

"Hello, Jo it's me again." I broadened my smile.

Jo smiled back with those Colgate white teeth.

"Jo I don't suppose you've got a hammer I could borrow?" I asked unaware of the shock of what I had just said would have on Jo.

"A hammer," Jo repeated his eyes widening into gigantic circles "Why you need a hammer for Mrs?"

"There's nothing to worry about, Jo," I started "Silly me, I've locked myself out of my car."

"What you want a hammer for Mrs?" Jo hadn't heard my last words.

"I've locked my keys in my car and need to break a window to get in," I said simply.

"I don't want no trouble Mrs." Jo's eyes narrowed.

"No no, Jo," I explained again, "I've locked myself out of my car and want to break in."

"No shit," Jo stared back at me, "No shit."

I wanted to say "No shit, just a hammer, Jo please," but thought better of it.

"Do you have a hammer, Jo?"

"Yes I's got a hammer, Mrs, but I don't want no trouble."

"No, I'll break the window. Could I borrow your hammer?" I was close to pleading.

Jo disappeared into the house, returning with a solid looking hammer, but before handing it over to me he once again had to say those immortal words that were beginning to sum up my day, "No shit." Or maybe it should have been 'loads of shit.'

Jo followed me the few paces to were my car was parked, watching me very carefully as I placed my hand bag, clip board and paperwork on the pavement.

"Mrs the man over de road breaks into cars for a living." Jo nodded to the scruffy house across the way, "He could get into de car in seconds."

"Into cars?" I questioned.

"Yeah you know, into cars, he a car thief," Jo said in a hushed tone so the fellow over the road didn't hear, not that he was anywhere to be seen.

"Oh I see," the penny dropped slowly.

I paused for a second. How would I phrase it if I was to go over and ask for the car thief's help? "Excuse me sir, I've been told you nick cars for a living. Silly me I've gone and left my keys in mine, would you mind using your skills to, well break into it." He would of course be thrilled to help, so pleased that I knew he was a car thief. Didn't take long for me to decide that one was a no no.

"It's OK, Jo," I said, taking the first swing at my driver's window. For whatever reason, this triggered Jo to commence some sort of Caribbean folk dance, as he jumped from one foot to the other, while chanting some oblivious ancient chant. "Oh shit," he said over and over again.

The hammer bounced off the window and out of my hand landing with a thud on my foot.

"Shit," I joined in with Jo.

"I'm not doing it Mrs," Jo assured me again.

"No it's OK Jo," I bravely smiled back, through the thumping pain that was starting in my toes, "I wouldn't expect you to."

Picking up the hammer, I noticed the blood trickling through the bar of my sandals. No more pussy footing about. If I dropped it again I'd look like a fool. Stepping back, looking like the man that introduces the Rank films at the cinema, but obviously far more attractive, I took a deep breath letting all hell lose with my full weight behind the blow. "Chink," said the car window at my pathetic effort, my hand ringing from the resounding blow I had just delivered. I knew what was coming.

"No shit." Jo repeated.

"Yes, Jo, no shit," was all I managed.

People break into cars every twenty seconds of every day. How difficult can it be?

My stance now resembled a pro golfer, feet apart I swung back with a force Jack Nicklaus would have been proud of. "Chink, chink, chink." The window gave in, allowing me as it did to put my hand through it.

"No shit," I heard as I retracted my hand from the broken window, blood pouring from the wound I had just acquired. It was competing with the blood oozing from my toes.

"There," I said with some satisfaction. "Thanks Jo." I handed back the now blood stained hammer.

"No shit Mrs," Jo beamed, as please as I was at my triumph.

I tried to clear away as much glass from the front seat so as to not to cause injury to my bum as well as my hand and toes. Jo returned to his house shaking his head as he went. He would, I think, put the incident down to British eccentricity.

I flung my hand bag, complete with essential stuff in it, which didn't include my phone or car keys, onto the back seat, my window completely bare. I would have to drive slowly.

At least the weather's good.

No sooner had this thought wandered through my mind did tiny rain drops begin to fall.

Not to worry. Another hour and I'll be home, I silently assured myself.

I turned onto the A140 toward Norwich, the wind blowing at me from the broken window, styling my hair into a sort of candy floss fashion which I was sure would never catch on. Those tiny droplets of rain now turned into a torrential downpour. By the time I hit Norwich's outer ring road, my lovely day in the sunshine had changed into hurricane Hannah. Gale force winds lashed at my little car, tunnelling through the broken window, hardly the rain fall they had forecast. I decided that if I reduced my speed to say twenty miles per hour, it would maybe help lessen the impact of the howling wind. The honking of horns from other motorists as they pulled out to pass me was a joy to hear. Some with heart warming gestures of two fingers, waving as they went, did little to deter me from my new found safety speed. No warp speed, Mr Sulu, for me.

"Good God Shelley." Peter asked questionably as I walked through the front door, dried blood on my hand and foot, my make-up resembling Alice Cooper, hair standing to attention. "What on earth happened?"

"Nothing. It's not been one of the best days," I grimaced back. "Sorry I broke the car window."

"Oh, OK." Peter knew when not to ask.

A tip given to me when I first began this job was by a seasoned interviewer called Elizabeth, which also involved glass, outlining the problems you can have with it. She warned or should I say advised me of an incident she had had when working.

"Never," she said, "Never knock on the panel of glass in a front door, or any door, come to that."

"Why?" I asked innocently.

"Well I did this job once, knocked on the glass panel." Her face was stern.

"And?"

"The whole bloody thing fell out," she said, without changing her expression, "I had to wait till the home owner came back to explain and offer to pay for the damage."

I still have to smile when I think of this, but now will never knock on a glass panel.

Some Guys Have All The Luck

I worked mostly for Cossett's, but now and then I would receive a phone call from other companies asking if I would work for them on a daily basis. Cossett's work was not always as varied as these other companies, so it was enjoyable to do something different from time to time. One company I occasionally worked for was Heart's Independent Survey's Ltd. I would be contacted by their local Supervisor to see if it was a job I would be interested in doing.

On a warm May evening with the sun still shining in a bright clear sky, Peter and I were working on our now slightly overgrown garden. There were no more of those blades of grass that saluted you as you walk past, no longer the straight trimmed edges of the lawn. My part time job as a market researcher had saved me from a lifetime of cutting mowing and pruning and digging. The garden now looked lived in, no longer a shrine to Home and Gardens. The daffodils stood with their heads brown and wilting.

"Phone," I heard Peter shout from somewhere under a nearby bush he was cutting back.

I walked towards the house, releasing my hands from those marigold gloves which seemed to want to become my second skin. In the end I gave up and left them on while I answered the phone.

"Hello?"

"Is Shelley there?" I heard Barbara's voice.

"Hello Barbara. It's me."

"Need you to cover a job. It's a lovely little one. You'll love doing it," Barbara announced.

I could picture her at the other end of the phone. She was seventy-five and had been doing market research for the best part of forty years. She resembled the Queen Mum with her white hair, but didn't have the yellowing teeth, rather the same majestic benevolence that you had to respect. She dressed always in a pleated skirts accompanied with neat twin sets always in lavender shades, she resembled a sweet little old lady. But there the resemblance stopped. Barbara took no prisoners, never took no for an answer, always had what she called "lovely little jobs." Should you dare to have the nerve to tell her that you were unable to work for her because you already had a job, the phone would be slammed down. Then the next time when she called having yet another "lovely little job" the grace and charm would be in full flow, no mention of the abrupt ending to any previous conversations.

"I know you'll love it. It's a lovely little job," Barbara repeated. "Have you got the next six weekends free?"

"Six weekends?" I stupidly questioned.

"Yes, dear: six. Now pop these dates in your diary," Barbara commanded.

Without thinking, I dutifully picked up my dairy which sat next to the phone and began filling in the dates Barbara dictated to me.

"I'll send you the locations and paperwork. It's a Government survey. They want to check on the usage of bridle paths. That's what you'll be doing, interviewing the folk that walk along. Just getting their impressions of the upkeep you know the sort of thing. Take that husband of yours along with you. They'll pay for him to chaperon you as some of the locations are a bit off the beaten track. Have a picnic. Make a day of it. It's a lovely little job." With that the phone was dead, Barbara was gone no doubt already dialling her next interviewer – or should I say loyal subject.

"Peter," I called as I struggled with my inside out marigold, blowing into it, hoping that it would assist in my endeavour to get the fingers out of the palm bit.

"Yeah?" I heard from the talking bush.

"Got you a job," I laughed.

Peter's head poked out between the Laural leaves. "What?"

"Don't worry," I smiled repeating Barbara's words. "It's a lovely little job."

The following day the paperwork arrived, complete with map showing the vicinity of where the bridle paths were. A smile crossed my face. Barbara must have posted them the morning before she had even asked me, knowing that I would be unable to refuse her royal command. But she was right. It was a lovely little job. All we had to do was turn up a six different locations each Sunday, wait for the passing ramblers, ask them about ten questions about what they thought of the surrounding area and what they thought of the upkeep. Basically that was it. Easier than tossing a pancake. And pay was wonderful £100 for me per day and £30 for Peter for watching over me, protecting me from harm.

Sunday arrived. Peter thought the idea of getting £30 was great. Working for himself for so many years, he giggled at the thought of having a pay packet.

"Ten percent for my agent fee," I demanded, as we piled the fold-down chairs and panic hamper into the back of the car.

"Sod off," Peter mocked. "I have been commissioned to protect thee, me lady for the princely sum of £30. That be my duty," he said, looking over his Ray Ban sunglasses, positioned at the tip of his nose.

It was a beautiful summer day and there was not a cloud in the sky as we followed the twists and turns of the country lane. The car radio, tuned to the local station, played Mary Wells *My Guy*.

"Nothing you can do," I sang, looking over to Peter. "Nothing you can say can take me away from My Guy."

"My Girl," Peter joined in.

"Think it's over there." I peered over my own sunglasses. "That looks like an opening."

Peter indicated, turning down the next left, following the directions I gave him from my highlighted map.

"Just pull over. Does this look like the right field?" I said holding the map at arm's length, trying to focus without changing to use my reading glasses.

"Yeah I think you right," Peter agreed, obviously thrilled that I hadn't done my usual trick of getting us lost.

Pulling on to the open path next to the field, Peter checked that everything was off. It was a routine he always had: car radio, indicator arm down, seat adjustment back to enable him to get his legs out of the car. His routine usually niggled me. It was the engineer in him. He had to double check everything. But not today it was too nice a day to worry about such things.

Undoing my door, I threw my legs out of the car and felt the warmth slip in between the toes as it engulfed my new flip flops. Looking down I knew what had happened, as I could now smell the aroma of cow dung as it proceeded to ooze its soft gooiness over both my feet.

"Oh God," I snorted, inexplicably deciding to shake one foot, flinging lumps of cow pooh into the air, watching as it completed the most basic of Newton's theory, arriving back on my lap, landing on my Marks and Spencer's non crease, shake dry slacks. "Oh God," I repeated. My Dad had always said you shouldn't take the Lord's name in vain and this was my punishment.

Stretching my neck to look back at Peter, I saw he had his hand over his mouth to stifle the laughter.

"It's not funny you old bugger." I forced the laughter out of my voice.

"I'm sorry, Shelley." Peter couldn't contain the gulps of laughter any longer. "Are you alright?"

"Like you sound as if you care," I said joining in with the now hysterical howls coming from Peter's direction. "Don't just stand there. Find me something to wipe this stuff off."

While I sat with my feet hovering above the obvious new and recent slushy cow pat, no crust having yet had time to form on it, I heard Peter rummaging around in the car boot, looking for a bit of old cloth to wipe my feet with.

"Hurry up," I shouted at the hatchback window.

Peter emerged from the back of the car holding my beloved tartan checked blanket we had bought last year when we toured Scotland.

"That's no good," I blasted back at him.

"Well that's all there is," he said, placing the beautiful square blanket inches away from the cow pat and my feet.

"There must be something else. Have another look." The funniness of the situation was wearing thin.

"Shelley, there's nothing else, I'm telling you." Peter held out a hand to help me out of the car. "It'll wash."

"But it's my tartan blanket," I said taking his hand.

"It'll wash Shelley come on," he repeated pulling me towards him.

As I stepped onto my beautiful tartan rug, leaving my new flip flops behind still engulfed in the cow pat, I tugged on Peter's hand, pulling him towards me, his grasp faltered causing the tip of his open toe sandal to joining my flip flop in the not so sweet smelly brown sludge.

"Careful Shelley" He said gaining his balance.

"Sorry." I murmured before letting out a gulp of laughter.

"It's not funny, Shelley." Peter was now wiping his sandal on the edge of the rug, leaving me to find my own way to an upright position.

"I didn't do it on purpose. Anyway, you parked here." A twinge of anger rose in me.

How come it was funny a moment ago when it was me in the shit, but not funny now?

Sitting on the grass in silence, both tugging at a corner of the tartan rug in an effort to wipe off the brown substance, I noted that although my feet were dry, they were now a light shade of brown from my ankles to my toes. Flip flops now discarded in the surrounding hedge row, I began to see the funny side again.

"Well at least you don't look like you've been tramping brown grapes to make wine," I giggled.

"No," Peter giggled back, "but we both smell country ish."

I had to agree there. The day was going to be a hot one, maybe not a good idea to try and interview member of the public smelling like a well fertilised field.

"Do you want to go home and change?" Peter asked.

"No better not, we should have been here half an hour ago," I replied. "I don't like to let Barbara down. But if you could find some water from somewhere so I can wash my feet, that'd be great."

"I'll get the chairs out. Maybe there's a pond somewhere about. If not will go and try and find somewhere that sells big bottles of water. You'll be alright on your own?"

"Yes course I will," I smiled at my knight in shining armour.

Peter positioned the folding chairs at the rear of the car, placing the larger panic box next to my chair then wrapping the tartan rug into a ball throwing it into the back of the car.

"I'll be back in a little while," he smiled "I'll have a walk down there, could be a pond or something."

"OK darling," I beamed back. "See you in a while."

As my intrepid explorer set off, I settled down with clip board at the ready beside me, opening my paperback. All was not lost. It was going to be a lovely hot summer day – a day in the country side.

After reading the first paragraph of my newest purchase, I felt the drizzle of warm fluid run down the back of my neck. Without thinking, I felt where the wet feeling had come from, turning slightly as I did so. It was then her eyes met mine. They were soft and brown. My own were white with terror.

"God," I screamed.

"Moo," she answered back

Staggering, I knocked my chair backwards in an attempt to put as much distance between her and myself.

"Moo," she said again, obviously unaware of the heart attack she had just given me.

"Stay there," I shouted, hoping she was an English-speaking cow. "Stay there. Peter! Peter!" I screamed, franticly looking round for my hero.

"Stay there," I repeated walking backward.

Undeterred, she ambled towards me, showing me how her large tongue could lick the end of her nose, a party trick I had never managed. "Moo."

"Stay there, nice cow," I stupidly uttered

I now had a new best friend. She just kept coming towards me, obviously thrilled to see someone visiting her field.

I was now edging my way towards the car, one arm outstretched to warn her off, "Nice cow," I repeated. "Good cow."

She seemed to like this compliment, and kept ambling her way towards me. Maybe she wanted to complete a survey.

Once at the car door I pulled on the handle: locked. Peter had locked the car.

Why!?!

Edging my way round the car, I tried to open the passenger door. Of course, Mr Engineer had locked it.

"I'll kill him," I vowed under my breath. "Just as soon as he's rescued me, I'll kill him."

"Peter," I shouted. "Peter, help me."

But my hero was off wandering the country side looking for water.

Did Jane have these sorts of problems with Tarzan? I think not.

Nice Cow looked over in my direction, probably wandering why her new found friend was shouting out to someone who was obviously not around and frantically pulling on a car door which was clearly locked. Thankfully, Nice Cow became bored after a few minutes. Unimpressed that her newfound friend was acting like a fruit cake, she turned, swished her tail in a good bye gesture, and wandered toward the other side of the field.

I gave myself a moment to gather my composure. I took a quick glance round, praying silently that no one had been watching the events of the last few minutes. Grateful that this bridle path was empty at this time of the day, I cursed that Peter had not been there in my moment of need.

"Peter?" I called again. "Peter where are you" I hollered at the top of my lungs then thought better of it in case my new friend Nice Cow thought I was calling to her.

"Typical," I hissed under my breath. "Now I've got to go find him."

We had decided not to take our phones. We didn't think we'd need them because we were to sit together for the day, relaxed and care free - released from those daily necessities that bugged our normal working lives. Of course, I couldn't complain. It had been my bright idea to leave them at home.

Walking through an open corn field, I had thoughts of a leggy blonde with flowing hair, delicate feature and, of course, those elegant bare feet. I've seen these kinds of things on adverts and at the movies. I've read about them in romantic novels. A handsome hero appears from nowhere and they embrace. Their lips touch. It's just shear poetry. Not so, I promise you.

Plodding through the open field I was mindful of the cow pat at every turn. The not so delicate smell from my stained feet was getting stronger in the rising heat of the day. Beads of sweat were now appearing on my furrowed brow, and my armpit was also wet from the trudging through open sun kissed fields. Nothing at all like Sting's song *Among the Fields of Barley*. All I could do was hope that "as he laid her down on that summers day", he cleared away all the sharp thistles and stinging nettles that lay hidden from view, the same ones which I was having no problem finding, cursing as I did.

"Shelley, Shelley," I heard Peter's voice

"Peter, Peter," I called back.

"Shelley," I could hear him but he was nowhere in sight. "Over here."

"Peter, where are you?"

"Down here." I looked in the direction of his voice. "Be careful it's steep."

"Keep talking so I can find you," I call back to him.

Following the sound of his voice, I walked towards a small clump of woodland.

"Peter," I called again.

"Down here," a small voice sounded.

Standing at the steep edge of what must have once been the sides of a extremely deep stream, I saw Peter, waist deep in water.

"Be careful, it's really slippery," he warned me, "I slipped in and the side are too steep to clamber out. Go and get help."

"Where from?"

"Christ, Shelley." Peter shouted up at me. "A farm, anywhere."

"I'll be back," I heard my voice say, but I didn't sound like Arnie out of *Terminator*. I sounded scared as I turned to run across the three-hundred acres wood.

"Keys," I said returning out of breath, after only two minutes or so.

"Keys?" Peter said bewildered.

"You've got the keys."

Peter fumbled in his pocket. "Catch," he shouted throwing them toward me with his full force.

Splosh! They fell with all the grace a bunch of keys could possibly have, into the murky waters of the once vibrant steam.

I looked at Peter and he looked at the ripple of rings spreading out across the water at the point the keys had entered, shaking his head in disbelief.

"Don't worry, I'll find someone," I reassured him as I turned to run to find a nearby homestead.

It felt like I had been travelling for several days when I finally saw the farm.

Please let someone be there to help, I silently prayed.

God had forgiven me for my past cursing. Farmer Giles was standing by the cattle shed, God bless him.

Farmer Giles scratched his head, dislodging his cloth cap as I ranted about our dilemma.

"OK my dear, you lead the way. We'll see what we can do," he said a bit too calmly for my liking, "You does market research does yer?"

Had I mentioned that in my rambling? Must have. Did he have to take an interest now, my beloved husband, the one who locks car doors for no apparent reason, was, as we spoke, floundering in a bog. I needed this man to act quickly. He walked me over to a barn at a pace Dillon out of the Magic Roundabout would have thought a trifle slow, opening the barn door to display a vintage tractor.

"Space for us both," he indicted to the door, pushing me up onto the high step, his hand flatly placed on my bum. God was I getting into an aged tractor with a pervert.

Never mind. No time to worry. I must save Peter.

Trundling our way through the beautiful English countryside on Farmer Giles tractor, I saw him glancing at my brown stained feet. I just couldn't muster the energy to explain. I was grateful that he didn't seem to mind the odour coming from them in the full heat of the day, in the closed space.

After what seemed like a lifetime sitting next to Farmer Giles, we arrived at the spot where my beloved was trapped.

Farmer Giles was not the village idiot I had pigeon-holed him to be. He knew exactly what to do once we arrived at the steep embankment.

Within half an hour, Peter was standing next to me in the open field, shaking Farmer Giles hand, truly thankful for his aid. We then took a quick trip back to the farm, passing Nice Cow along the way as she happily grazed with some of her other four legged friends, apparently not at all bothered that I didn't stop to exchange pleasantries with her.

Farmer Giles and his lovely wife Lorretta, allowed us to call our son Lawrence, refusing any payment for their kindness of using their phone. We gave the briefest of explanations to Lawrence. They were more like straight forward commands: go to our house, get the spare keys for the car, and drop them off without stopping at the pub for a swift half.

A cuppa offered from Lorretta was gratefully accepted. Her and her husband both didn't seem in the least bit fazed by this odd couple standing before them. Offering food if we wanted some, which we declined. They gave Peter a pair of trousers they had put aside for the scarecrow, which miraculously fitted him – well all but the length. The saying "Put some jam in your shoes and invite your trousers down to tea" applied, as they finished about three inches from his ankles. The Giles couple seemed to take everything in their stride. They were Norfolk's answer to Ma and Pa Larkin. Thanking them yet again we left, once Lawrence had arrived with the spare keys.

"Why are your feet brown, Mum?" Lawrence asked. "And what's that funny smell?"

"Don't ask," I growled back.

"Your mother's had a long day." Peter said in my defence.

"Were did you get those trousers from Dad?" Lawrence grinned.

Lawrence took note of our faces, thought better of continuing to ask questions, and drove us to our car.

Once in the car, Peter turned the ignition on. The car radio blurted out *Some Guys Have All The Luck* by Rod Stewart. It broke the stony silence. Peter glanced over to me. I smirked and he giggled.

"That was worth thirty quid," he grinned.

Telephoning Barbara that evening, I began to come out with some sort of explanation, leaving out most of the truth. I told her how I couldn't accept payment as I hadn't completed a single interview.

"No my dear, you're not alone. All my ladies today found it difficult. No one seems to use the bridle paths. At least you were good enough to go along and sit there all day." Barbara laughed. "Maybe we'll have more luck over the next five weeks."

Before I could argue further Barbara had gone and Peter had appeared in the hallway, holding two glasses of wine. I didn't have the heart to mention that we had a further five weekends of surveys to complete on bridle paths, but we would at least take our phones with us, and I would take a spare set of keys.

Bench People

Bench people are present in every town or city I have ever worked in. These groups usually congregate on the seating provided by the local council. They sit watching the world go by. None appear to have jobs. They can often be heard telling each other about their different experiences in prison, or some other institution they have frequented at some time or another. There are no holds barred in their language, which is more than colourful. They never speak in hushed tones and the air can turn blue if you stand close to by.

In Norwich the bench people consists of a whole family, from babes in arms to Gran and Granddad taking up their rightful seat on the benches provided. I caught a conversation between the Grandmother and her Granddaughter one overcast morning in July. I tried to be discrete while eavesdropping as I edged a little closer to catch each detail.

"Well it's all fucking changed now, not like it was when I went in," the Grandmother spouted at her Granddaughter, armed folded across her ample belly. "The screws knew where they stood and we knew how far we could push our fucking luck. Not like nowadays."

"You can't even get burn allowance if you don't have a job," the Granddaughter joined in.

"Fucking disgraceful." Grandmother shook her head in horror.

"Then they only lets you have two fucking ounces a week," said Granddaughter as she pushed an unwanted dummy at her toddler sitting in a pushchair. "Wot if they does'nt give you a fucking job? You're fucked."

I realised they had moved their glare from each other, looking over in my direction with a look of distaste. Glaring at this woman, clip board in hand obviously listening to their conversation, I smiled at them. The Grandmother was now eyeing me from head to toe still with the look of disgust on her face.

"Morning," I said feebly, but got nothing in return. I decided then it was time to inch away from the spot where I had planted myself.

I gathered from the snippet I had heard that both had been in prison, the granddaughter perhaps recently. The "burn" they were referring to was tobacco that the Granddaughter, while serving her time to repay her debt to society, had been unable to get. I decided I had had a sheltered upbringing.

We don't ever try to recruit any of the bench people maybe because most of us are, if the truth be told are a little afraid of the response we might get. I guess also because we believe, maybe wrongly, that they might not be able to complete a survey by themselves, especially if it is a self completion on a laptop. Also we are supposed to recruit members of the public with a little bit of intelligence, again wrongly or rightly we all suppose these people have none. However, on a day when you're struggling to get people the temptation to recruit 'anyone' is difficult to resist, which my friend and colleague Jenny found out to her cost.

While working in Peterborough, the job in hand was having to recruit fifty six people from all walks of life. With so many males, so many females, all ages from fourteen years old to seventy five years young, the day was proving difficult. By two o'clock we had only filled half the quota required, most of those being **ABC1** (professional or white collar workers) we were desperate to some **C2DE's** (skilled workers, non skilled workers and those out of work).

All five of us working that day had only achieved five or six recruited respondents each. We had to achieve eleven apiece to get the job done.

Jenny walked towards me. "Have you noticed anything different with that lot?" she nodded towards the bench people.

I glanced over in their direction to discover that each and every single one of them had dyed their hair jet black. Not only that. They looked a strange yellow colour. It became obvious that they must have made a bulk purchase of self tanning lotion as well as the hair colour. Rather than looking silky tanned, they all looked as if they had suffered a sudden attack of yellow jaundice. Their faces were all streaky. Sadly, even the baby, aged about six months, also had jet black hair and yellow stained skin. I had to turn away at this point having fallen into a fit of giggles, which Jenny, knowing my sense of humour knew I would.

"They look like a band of outlawed Mexicans," Jenny giggled.

"Don't," was all I managed before making a sniffled snorting noise.

We plodded on with the recruiting, taking the refusals with a smile. I had to make a determined effort not to look over in the direction of the bench people, knowing I would break down in hysterical laughter again.

"God, this is hard work today," Jenny muttered. "Bit like pulling teeth."

"Yeah," I agreed with her.

"Well we could always recruit the bench people,'" Jenny said with a grin.

"You first, if you've got that much energy," I said.

We went on, but no one would stop. It just seemed to get worse.

"Bugger this," Jenny announced, "bench people it is." And with that she walked toward the area of seating and without hesitation, went into, "Excuse me. We're conducting some market research. Would you be willing to take part in a survey?"

I watched in disbelief, praying that she would come to no harm and leave the scene with all her limbs still in tacked. Armed, ready with my clip board to rush in, break up any fight that might occur, I was ready to help my friend in her foolish moment as she abandoned her common sense.

"Yeah we'll do it," said one of the yellow bench people, standing up, nodding at his fellow companions – his silent instruction for all of them to follow his example.

Jenny looked over her shoulder and winked at me as she led her newly recruited band of streaky yellow respondents toward the venue. She would need help so I followed her in disbelief, as did the rest of the team. Like lambs to the slaughter we followed her, some of us with open mouths still not grasping fully what she had done.

Once in the venue, all hell broke loose. Trying to get all seven of the bench people seated at each laptop turned out to be a new and different experience. Bodies seemed to be everywhere in that tiny room. I sat the youngest member of the group, a young girl of sixteen down and explained what was required. She seemed to understand without much instruction, using the mouse to enter her details on the screen.

"If you need any help, there's always one of us in the room. Just shout out," I said as I stood up to leave her to complete the survey by herself.

"They had fucking computers inside. I'll be alright," she said with a class of refinement all of her own

Looking round the room I decided to help further by making teas and coffees for this bulk recruitment of Jenny's.

Asking each of them in turn what their preferred drink would be seemed to trigger off a huge discussion. It seemed to be a difficult decision to make. One of them asked if we had anything stronger, looking slightly disappointed when I told them we didn't and finally deciding on coffee with six sugars.

Jenny had seated the chap she had originally recruited outside in front of the laptop, but she seemed to be having some difficulty making him fully understand what he had to do. The computer had selected a survey on toothpaste for him after Jenny had entered the first lot of information for him. The initial question he had to answer was, "Do you have any or all of your own teeth?" This seemed to totally throw him.

"Do you have all or some of your own teeth?" Jenny asked.

"I don't know, luv, do you?" he came back at her.

"No. Do *you* have all or some of your teeth?" Jenny asked again.

"What der you mean luv?" he replied not taking his glare from the screen.

"They're asking, do you have all or some of your natural teeth?" Jenny said patiently

"I knows how to make a cuppa tea. Did it in occupational therapy." He was stuck in the glare of the bright lights coming from the computer screen.

"Oh," Jenny stared back at him, somewhat taken aback by his reply. "But do you have all or some of your natural teeth?"

"How do I know if you've got natural teeth," he answered sincerely.

"No, do YOU have natural teeth?" Jenny said leaning in front of him, bearing her own beautiful nashers as she pronounced each word slowly.

He raised his glare from the screen, slowly looked towards Jenny then was drawn back to the laptop. "Is this about teeth then?" he asked.

"Yeah, do you have all or some of your natural teeth?"

"Oh they want to know do I have all my own teeth?" he asked.

"Yes," Jenny let out a sigh of relief "Do you?"

There was a moment of silence. You could almost hear the clogs going round as he pondered on this important question. "I don't know," came his reply.

Jenny's shoulders sagged, but with the strength of a true market researcher, she asked again, "Are your teeth your own?"

He turned, facing Jenny, bewilderment on his face. He opened his mouth for Jenny to inspect the content there in.

Jenny peered in. "Yes you've got two at the back." She sounded triumphant. "So the answer is yes."

"Right," he said, looking back at the laptop.

"So you put in yes," Jenny pointed to the correct answer on the screen.

"Right," he agreed with her, sitting stiller than a breeze block.

"So you touch the yes answer on the screen," Jenny advised him.

"Right, I see." He agreed, but made no move.

There was nothing for it, Jenny picked up his hand in which he was clutched the pointing pencil leading it towards the yes button. "There. Yes," she said to almost reassure herself as much as him.

"Right, I see," he said again.

"Now touch the 'continue' bar there," Jenny said, helping his hand toward the huge blue bar at the bottom of the page to enable to the next page to be displayed.

"Right, I see," he agreed.

"And how often do you visit the dentist?" Jenny asked the next question.

"How would I know how often you visit the dentist?" he asked.

"No." Jenny began, "How often do YOU visit the dentist?"

It was at this point I couldn't watch any longer. This one wasn't going to be a self completion. Jenny was going to have to stay with him throughout the survey. Day light might have gone before she would be outside again.

I looked over at my colleagues helping the other bench people settle into their own surveys. All of them seemed to be having as much trouble as Jenny. The only one getting on with it was my sixteen year old.

Julie and another colleague had sat one of the older women at a laptop. She was struggling to get her to answer each question. As she answered each question, she would holler at the top of her lungs, "Is that it luv?"

Julie patiently explained that there were a few more question to answer, but still, after each one was answered, she was still asked, "Is that it luv?"

I decided to get out while I could. The noise was deafening.

An hour or so later, the bench people emerged from the venue, each clutching their latest possession and the free give away pen each respondent received as a token of thanks for taking part in the survey.

"Thanks for the pen," I heard one of them shout back through the door.

Jenny and the others followed shortly afterwards, looking battle scarred and emotional drained.

"Well at least we got seven C2DE's." Jenny tried to sound positive.

"Shut up Jenny," we shouted back.

Nice Doggie

Ninety nine percent of the people we interview are the nicest, kindest people on God's good earth – well, maybe eighty-nine percent. They are happy to give up twenty minutes of their time to not only help you complete your job but to also give their opinions on whatever subject we are working on. Once stopped in the street the most common reply if they agree to take part in the survey is, "Oh, go on then. If it'll help you". It's a personality thing I guess. Same thing applies to door to door surveys. You are there knocking on their front door asking to be invited in to their homes. For all they know, you could be anyone. It takes some trust to let a perfect stranger in to your home. I still can't get over the fact that people are kind enough to do so. These people are "Salt of The Earth" types. It's sometimes not them that is the problem, rather their additional family or the family pets, those furry or feathered friends that they consider are included as part of their family.

When my children were small, we did the 'Pet' thing. We had every imaginable pet, ranging from dogs to cats, gerbils to rabbits. We even at one time kept stick insects, which the kids would race across the living room when I was feeling generous enough to let them out of their glass tank. Now there are only the two of us, we no longer feel the need to have a pet. That's not to say that I dislike animals. It's just a different time for us. I'm the first to smile at some little dog with a cute face, but that's as far as it goes.

When doing a door to door survey, hearing the bark or howl of a dog, coming from inside the house, has the effect of, "Please let it be friendly and well behaved." They may be the owner's best friend, but will they be friendly towards a market researcher? I know some market researchers that will leave the doorstep before anyone answers if they hear a dog behind the door. I have done surveys in houses, with certain breeds of dog which terrify me, one of those being a Bull Staffordshire Terrier. They always seem edgy, plus it's difficult to concentrate if you have this four legged creature standing inches away from you, not moving its stare from you. You hear of these pets even turning on their owners, or even worse the children of the household. Why would you take a chance?

All market researchers have some tale or another about a household pet. The one that sticks in my own mind happened to myself and a supervisor.

Mary had telephoned me to ask if I was available to join her for my appraisal – what we call an IPR, something which is undertaken once a year to keep in line with the strict Market Researchers Code of Conduct. A supervisor, such as Mary, comes along with you to check you're doing everything correctly.

"Is that date OK?" she asked me on the phone.

"Yes of course. Where do you want to meet?"

"The local police station," Mary suggested. "The one near ASDA."

"Fine I'll see you there," I concluded.

If you are working a door to door it is a requirement that you register at a local police station. This does two things. It ensure that someone knows roughly where you are in case you go missing, or if someone calls the police thinking you are stalking the neighbourhood, at least there is an explanation why you are there.

I met Mary at the appropriate time and we signed in at the police station. Once outside she asked me which area I wanted to work in.

"Don't mind, Mary. Do you want me to lead the way? You follow me and when I see an estate we can work I'll turn off."

"Sounds good to me," she smiled.

We travelled a few miles and I saw what I thought would be a good place to start. Once we'd parked our cars Mary explained she would have to do the first interview, supposedly to show me how do the job correctly.

"Yeah that's fine," I agreed.

We walked along the road, exchanging small talk about our kids and what sort of work we'd both recently done, stopping our conversation only when we stood outside a door having rung the bell and waiting for the resident to answer. After a few polite, "No thanks" we walked up the path of a large well kept garden – well kept, apart from several large holes littering the neatly kept lawns. Both of us noticed them at the same time.

"Looks like they tried to pull up some large trees," Mary noted.

Pressing the door bell, we listened for the chimes to ring out. Ding Dong they rang out, followed by what sounded like a small pony with its hoofs pounding along the hallway of the house. Then came the furious barking of the house owner's loving "pet". With each howl the animal threw its body against the door – fling itself against it with the force of a wildebeest. Mary glanced at me, her face looking whiter than mine. I nodded at her, she understanding my gesture of let's get out of here before they answer. We both turned, now in a race against time, towards the open garden gate we had just entered moments before.

"Yes, can I help you?" came the voice from the now open door.

Come on, Mary. Just say no we've made a mistake, wrong address, think of something quick. I tried to project my thoughts towards Mary.

Mary turned, facing house owner standing with the doorway ajar, her left hand holding back the slobbering hound who obviously wanted to have lunch by eating one of us then maybe bury the other one in one of those holes where a tree had once stood, for a snack later on.

"Sorry to disturb you."

That's the idea, Mary. Good start.

"But we're doing some market research in the area and wondered if you could help complete a survey."

I stood looking at her in disbelief.

"Oh yes, of course I will, do come in." the woman said, staining to control the dog. "Down Celia," she said.

Please God let her add, "I'll just put Celia in the back room".

"Don't mind Celia, she's just playful," she smiled as her left arm holding Celia was wrenched from its socket, Celia bounded forward to greet us or eat us.

"Lovely, thank you." Mary stepped forward, ignoring my glare.

Celia, full of the joys of spring, and thrilled to be released, bounded up to Mary, leaping at her, front paws placed squarely on Mary's shoulders. Celia began lovingly licking all Mary's face make-up off.

"She loves meeting new people," Celia's owner beamed.

As Mary was unable to speak, due to the fact Celia seemed to be French kissing her, I agreed on her behalf. "We can see that," I said.

Once inside the house Celia's proud owner commanded her to sit. Celia was having none of it. She ignored every command uttered by her. "Sit Celia, that's a good girl," she tried, as Celia showed us how she could bound around the room at top speed, knocking things over as she went.

"Celia, stop showing off," her proud owner smiled lovingly at her pet. Now Celia, after thoroughly having cleaned Mary's face, decided it was my turn. She pushed her large bony face into mine.

"Down you get," I said in my strict voice, pushing her back. Celia gazed at me with an almost hurt expression, then must have decided I wasn't her type and went back to loving Mary.

The house was shall we say, different. The sitting room was dedicated to the love of all things great and small. Celia was now being controlled by her loving mistress' firm grip, in a bid to try and prevent her from licking Mary to death. The floor was covered in sheets of newspaper and all the seating had fake fur-covered throws with yellow stains dotted here and there. I stood wondering where I could plonk my bottom, not wishing to sit in what was clearly doggy wee. Without warning, a pussy cat appeared from under one of the sofas and began to wrap its self around my legs purring happily at the sensation. I noticed that the poor little thing only had one eye. Near the fire place two badly stuffed cats sat peering with eyes that seemed to go in different directions. I wondered if one of those eyes had belonged to pussy who was twisting round and round my legs, then dismissed such an evil thought. Every ornament was dedicated to God's wonderful creation. A small oak table to the left of the fireplace was covered in every manner of sculpture of woodland birds. Figurines of all descriptions of cats and doggies covered every available space on the window sill, mantle piece and shelving behind the sofa. A large parrot cage hung from a ceiling hook with as far as I could calculate four or five small buggies enclosed there.

A slight rustling noise drew my attention to the corner of the room. Gazing over I noticed a wood framed box with several partitions dividing it into three sections. Each section contained a different species of mammal, one contained three miniature bunnies, happy in their shredded newspaper. The second I noticed with some alarm had two white, rats their tails resembling ground worms. Now I don't mind doggies, bunnies, cats, but rats are something of a terror for me. I found myself transfixed by them. Checking the wooden box to see if there was any route of escape for these creatures, I found the third compartment empty.

"Do take a seat," Celia's mistress offered.

"Thanks," said Mary, not taking due care where she sat, while I perched on the edge of a chair, checking for yellow stains, pussy still circling my ankles. "This is my college, Shelley. We're working together today."

"Hello, Shelley," Celia's mistress nodded. "Hope you don't mind animals."

"No, of course not," Mary smiled, arranging her clip board so as to commence the interview, not noticing the fear on my face as I watched the rats scurrying around in their wooden cell.

"Now Celia," Celia's mistress announced in a condescending voice as she leaned towards Celia's ear, "These nice ladies have come to see us today to do a survey, I want you to behave."

I just hoped Celia spoke English.

"So Mummy is going to let go now and I want you to be a good girl."

Instead of trying to reason with this oversized creature, why doesn't she put the damn thing outside, just while we were here? The rats could go with her. They could have a party in the garden, away from us.

"Her bark's worse than her bite," Celia's mistress assured us as she released Celia, "Be good girl now."

Free at last, the dog shook her huge head, her floppy chops swaying from side to side as she enjoyed her newly gained freedom. The film *Turner and Hooch* sprang to mind as spit and slobber from Celia's mouth sprayed the room, landing with large splats on the newspaper covered floor, as well as Mary and myself. Celia, overjoyed at the chance to make a new friend, bounded yet again in my direction, throwing her ample paws onto my lap, pinning me back into the chair. Her large head inches away from my face, I managed to restrain the scream I wanted to let out, but my eyes were wider than the a black hole.

"Now what did Mummy tell you? Bad girl. Down you get,"

Celia's Mistress commanded with little reaction from Celia as she progressed to slobber onto my top, while I sat pinned to the chair. "Down you get, you just have to tell her firmly."

How can I be firm with her when my arms are pinned to the sides of my body?

I was too scared to move in case Celia remembered me pushing her away the first time and decided to bite my head off. I gave a pleading glance toward Mary. This gesture was wasted. Being the true professional, Mary was ready to undertake the interview, although I felt sure she was smirking.

"Now as, I said we're conducting a survey. Can I just check a few details with you?"

Mary this maybe my IPR you're checking on me, but I am going to get you after school, I silently promised.

Celia now seemed bored with the petrified woman who would not acknowledge her. Jumping down from my lap, she turned her head, which was the size of a prize winning pumpkin, toward Mary. Maybe Celia had spied that there were papers to ruffle, much better game than a boring woman who just sat there staring back at her. With one tremendous leap, she cleared the distance between the armchair where I was seated, landing with great satisfaction directly in front of Mary stopping only for a minute's hesitation before nuzzling her head between Mary's legs.

Mary let out a tiny scream, but not to be deterred she pulled clipboard with associated papers, out from under Celia's head and proceeded with the interview.

God that women should win Professional of the Year, I thought.

Half way through the interview, Celia's mistress asked if we would like a drink, to which we both replied a bit too hastily that we were fine.

"Well I'll just pop and make myself a coffee if that OK."

Mary looked over to me as she left the room.

I didn't know what to say.

"Help me," Mary uttered as she strained with both hands to lift Celia's head from its position on her lap.

"Then I'll have her on mine," I selfishly said.

"Shelley, help me." Mary was desperate.

I stood up, walking very gingerly toward Mary and the lovely Celia.

"Come on now, Celia" I coaxed as I placed both of my hands either side of Celia's enormous head.

Celia moved not one inch, as both Mary and I pushed and pulled, straining every muscle we possessed.

"Come on, Celia," I puffed.

"She's not going anywhere," Mary said dejectedly.

"You sure you don't want a drink?" Celia's mistress called from the kitchen.

"Thanks, we're fine," I said quickly returning to my seat, hoping that on her return she wouldn't notice how red-faced Mary and I were from all that puffing and panting.

Mary looked at me.

"Sorry," I shrugged.

Celia's mistress returned taking her seat next to Mary.

"Now where were we?" she said sipping her coffee. "Oh I nearly forgot," she added glancing at the cuckoo clock on the wall opposite. "It's time for Jade, Lucy, Mickey and Tony to have their constitutional. Hope you don't mind, but they'll never forgive me if I don't keep to the correct time."

She walked over to the open window, closing it as we looked on, both our minds racing as to who Jade, Lucy, Mickey and Tony were. After a few steps she was standing by the parrot cage, blowing kisses through the rungs.

"Come on my darling, out you come," Celia's mistress twittered, as she unlatched the cage door as Jade, Lucy, Mickey and Tony, who seemed to be standing in a orderly queue. taking turns in hopping through the open doorway. The four buddies took flight around the room. So pleased to have these moments of freedom, they swept over both mine and Mary's heads, showing us the expertise of a birdie's version of the Red Arrows.

I guess I was luckier than Mary. At least I could move a little more than she could, not having the restriction of Celia's head buried deep in my groin. Jade, Lucy. Mickey and Tony swooped this and that way over our heads, Celia's mistress letting out little shrieks of delight as they did so.

"Birds are so graceful," she uttered with simplistic joy.

Ungraciously, I wondered if I held my clip board up we'd be lucky enough for one of the birds to fly into it. Then they could join the two fireplace cats. I'd even offer to pay the taxidermist. "Yes, graceful," I said.

Mary continued to ask Celia's mistress the closing questions of the survey, while I now sat with either Jade, Lucy, Mickey – or was it Tony? – perched on the top of my head, praying against all odds that whoever it was wouldn't feel the call of nature. The other three sat behind me picking at the fabric of the chair I sat on. The fear of Alfred Hitchcock's film *The Birds* whirling through my mind.

"Well thank you so very much," Mary said making a tremendous effort yet again to remove Celia's head from her slobber saturated lap. "Here's a thank you note, just explains all about the company we work for." More straining noises from Mary as she pushed with all the strength a women of her build could muster. "Thank you again."

"That's' OK my dear." Celia's mistress stretched out to retrieve Celia's head. "Come on now Celia, it's time for these nice ladies to go."

Celia turned towards her mistress, eyes downcast at having to leave such a comfortable place.

"Um, will Jade, Lucy, Mickey and Tony be alright?" I said hopeful that she would also free me from my feathered captures.

"Just push them away dear. They'll be fine. Time they were going back anyway."

Thanking Celia's mistress once again, Mary and I rushed towards the front door.

"Pop back anytime," Celia's mistress shouted as we ran down the pathway, now realising the holes in the lawn were Celia's handy work.

"Mary, can we do this some other time?" I asked picking birdie pooh out of my hair. "I'm really not in the mood for an IPR."

"Yeah, I think that's a good idea," Mary said looking down at her wet slobber ridden clothing, "How about next week?"

"Yeah, sounds good," I agreed. "No more pets though."

"No, no pets," she nodded in agreement.

Never Judge A Book By Its Cover

Recruiting the public you are supposed to have an open mind. We all can assume things. You may think that a person who is well dressed is a professional person, but not so. I have approached many people out in their Sunday best only to have my initial preconception of their occupation shattered as they inform me that they are a refuge collector or out of work. Of course it can work the other way: you can approach someone dresses in thread bare clothes only to find that they work in a professional environment. It's difficult to rid yourself of these ideas. An open mind is called for at all times.

When interviewing someone I tend to play a game. As I ask a question I place a mental bet on what their answers will be. It's really wrong of me to pigeon-hole people in this way, but most times I guess right, stupidly grinning to myself at the time as if I'd gained a brownie point in my own imaginary quiz. My little game can lighten the only boring part of the job, reading out the same questions several times throughout the day.

Part of all surveys includes recording the verbatim of the respondent's opinion on either the advert we are testing or on the products itself. Not being a brilliant speller I live in dread of getting some clever dick who knows a load of posh words that I don't even understand let alone can spell. I also have a blind spot, when it comes to certain words or names, never can spell "sergeant" or for some unknown reason the name "Margaret".

I was working in Ipswich one freezing cold morning. It was the kind that makes you shake from top to toe. I was with four other members of the team recruiting in the street, talking to members of the public who were kind enough to stop in the fridge-like conditions and come to a venue to complete a survey on toothpaste. It wasn't a self completion survey this time but one with us asking questions and recording answers onto a laptop.

Toothpaste not being the most interesting subject, we thought it might be a struggle to recruit anyone, given the weather conditions as well. I approached my first respondent, "Excuse me, sir. We're conducting market research today. Would you be kind enough to take part in a survey?"

I looked straight into his eyes as I always did when trying to recruit. Good old eye contact works most times, but this man had the coldest eyes I have ever seen.

"And what young lady is the survey about?" he asked.

I truthfully answered, "Toothpaste," knowing that I shouldn't have divulged this information at this point.

Unprofessional Shelley, I reprimanded myself mentally.

"Toothpaste, I see. And what do you want to know about toothpaste?"

I couldn't put my finger on why this man made me feel uncomfortable, after all he had stopped on this coldest of days, hadn't been rude, was reasonable well dressed in a grey overcoat with his shoes polished to a high shine. There was just something about him. He had this air.

"We'd like you to err, err, err…"

Why am I stuttering?

"We'd like you to look at an advert then give us your opinion," I finally managed.

"And what makes you think that I would have an opinion, young lady?"

The whole "Young Lady" thing was now getting on my nerves, "Thank you for the young lady," I gave half hearted laugh.

"Well you are a young lady aren't you?" His tone made it clear this was not a rhetorical question.

"Would you be willing to take part in the survey?" I said hoping he would decline.

"As you have put it so eloquently, how can I refuse?" he glared back at me.

Running through the recruitment questions, I kept hoping that he would at some point not be eligible to take part, but of course he fitted the criteria.

Sod's law.

"The rest of the survey is in here," I said pointing to the entrance of the venue.

"Lead on, young lady." He made a swooping gesture with is arm.

"Thank you." I forced a smile.

Once in the venue I offered him a cup of coffee or tea.

"I won't, thank you." He answered politely but the feeling he gave me was he didn't fancy any drink I had made.

Sitting next to him, I began putting in the general information to begin the survey on the computer.

"Could you give me your name and address, sir?" I asked, poised and ready to type.

"And what are you going to do with this information, young lady?" His voice was as cold as the day outside.

"We don't pass on the data," I said truthfully. "It's just to check on us as interviewers that you are a real person and that we haven't made you up."

"Well, as you can see I am a real person." He risked a half smile.

"I know..."

Blimey. Maybe he is human after all.

"But as I said it's just to back check on us."

"I have your personal assurance that this information is not passed onto anyone else?" he double checked.

"I promise," I said handing him our standard thank you note. "There's a free phone number on here should you have any questions. It also explains about the data protection of all personal details."

Taking the thank you note he then began to read the information given. The feeling that he didn't trust what I had just said was very apparent.

"Very well. My name is Mr. Norman Jasper Fredrick Cuthbert-Howard," he said with pride.

I began typing, Norman Cuthbert-Howard.

"No, No, my name is not Norman Cuthbert-Howard. It is, as I just informed you Mr Norman Jasper Fredrick Cuthbert-Howard."

"We only need your first and surname, sir," I said pointedly.

"That you may. But my name is as I said, young lady," came his curt answer.

No point in arguing.

I began typing in his full name.

"No, no. This won't do. My name is Cuthburt-Howard," he stretched out his long index finger toward the screen. "Cuthburt with an 'u' not an 'e'."

"Sorry," I said correcting the spelling.

"It's a common mistake. But if we're going to do it, let's do it correctly." He watched the screen to ensure that I didn't make the same mistake twice.

The same thing happened with his address. He informed me he lived at "The Squirrels End, Munching Lane, Swaffham, Norfolk. Do you think I could remember how to spell squirrel? No of course not. Three attempts later, we got there.

Most of the survey was bog standard, but I took great care to listen to each of his responses, recording them with the precision of a brain surgeon.

"Now we'd like you to watch this advert," I said handing him the set of headphones.

He eyed the headphones with contempt, taking them from me after a few minutes of hesitation. Watching the advert of a very pretty girl brushing her already overly white teeth, his expression remained stone-like. He placed the headphones stoically on the table once the advert had completed.

"Have you seen this advert before?" I asked, clicking onto the next page of the survey on the computer.

"No," was his brief reply.

"Now we'd like to ask you some questions on the advert." I clicked with trepidation to the next page knowing that the next screen was where I had to record word for word his responses. "What did you like about the advert?"

"I felt that the gross impact was not only condescending to the vast numbers of those who would be influenced by such a translucent fabrication of this advertisement."

I pondered for a split second, wondering if I should ask, "But did you *like* the advert?" but I thought better of it. The dread of missing something he'd said was fresh in my mind. He would be sure to reprimand me if I got even the slightest thing wrong. I toyed with the idea of turning the screen away from him so I could just type, "Not a lot", but I knew I wasn't supposed to do that, and anyway, he would suss what I was up to.

Sighing, I set about my task. He watched as I struggled with the spelling of "influenced", my mind working over time, not only on the correct spelling, but that I'd put everything down in the right order.

"No, young lady, that's not how you spell 'influenced.'" Again, he pointed his long, bony finger at the screen.

He knew I was going to get it all wrong, knew I was thicker than an oak door. As I typed his response, he corrected me on each and every word.

"Thank you," I said, feeling like a five year old.

And so it went on.

The end of the survey in sight, I breathed a deep sigh of relief. "And finally, sir, so we collect a cross section of the public, can I ask the occupation of the chief income earner in the household?"

"That would be me, as I live on my own. I am a factory operative," was his reply.

To put it in my Grand Mothers words, you could have knocked me down with a feather. This man of many, many words most, of which I had no idea what they meant, let alone that they existed, worked on the factory shop floor, probably doing the most mundane tasks. At first glance I had had him down as a businessman maybe even a doctor. From the verbatim I had just recorded, with him helping me every step of the way, I had thought he was maybe a University Don. His posture, dress code and the way in which he made me feel more than a little inadequate did not give away his day time profession.

I had to ask, "Do you have any qualifications?"

"No, young lady, I left school at fifteen," he answered coolly.

I thanked him for his time, presented him with the token pen, saw him to the door and watched as he walked out into the cold winter day, swaggering as he went.

Putting on my coat, wrapping my scarf around myself in an attempt to keep out the cold, I thought of him sitting alone in his home, dictionary open. Did he do as Marilyn Monroe was said to have done, learn a new word each day, or in his case four or five? If he did he was to be admired, self education is a wonderful thing, If only he had been a bit more graceful about it. He had taught me a useful lesson, never judge a book by its cover, something else my Grandmother would always say. My Grandmother and I had something in common. Neither of us liked clever dicks, people who took pleasure in making other feel uncomfortable or inadequate.

Nice But, Not The Brightest Berry On The Bush

To every Ying there is a Yang. There are those who live content in their world. These people are happy to help you do a survey, always ready to please, but not the brigtest berry on the bush. They mean well but don't fully understand what is required of them. You can try and explain over and over again but nothing is ever absorbed.

Working in my home city of Norwich, the job requirement for that day was that the people recruited had to have travelled ten miles or more outside Norwich City Boundary. I still to this day cannot believe how many people we asked had not travelled that distance. Who am I to judge, if you don't need to or want to travel more than ten miles out, who am I to say you should? The survey was to be done on a laptop, this time a self completion.

We recruited the general public at street level, took them into the venue and explained that the laptop was a touch screen and that they just had to give their opinions on whatever topic the survey was about, in this case travel outside Norwich. Most questions were multiple-choice. They just had to point the touch pen at the screen and give their answers. Did they think the advert was interesting, boring, or dull, that sort of thing. Rocket science it wasn't. Really, nothing could be easier. Most people picked up the gist within two minutes – not so the couple I recruited on that autumn day.

My approach was as normal. "Excuse me, we're conducting market research. Would you be willing to take part in a survey?"

"What luv?" the elderly man asked.

"We're conducting market research. Would you be willing to take part and do a survey?"

"What you think, Maureen?" he said turning to his nicely rounded wife.

"I don't mind, George," she smiled back at him.

I asked them the very basic questions required for this type of survey. He was sixty three, she was fifty nine, (again I had pigeon holed them thinking they were much older, I have should learned by now,) They lived in the Anglia Region. He was the chief income earner, a glazier. They fitted into the criteria so I asked if they would continue, to which after a bit of discussion they agreed.

"There's a lot of steps," I warned them as we went through the doorway.

"Have to take it slow and steady then," he laughed.

By the time we had reached the room up the three flights of steps, Maureen was totally out of breath, although we had taken a good twenty minutes to reach the summit.

"Come on girl," George had encouraged her on the upward climb.

"I'm alright," she replied as she struggled with the next step.

"Takes it out of you." I paused to wait for Maureen, thinking that she was only two years older than me.

"Hmm," she managed plodding on.

Once in the room they saw the dreaded laptops.

"Oh no, George I can't use one of them." Maureen's fear of using technology apparent.

"Promise you it's ever so easy. They make it easy for us," I joked, trying to make Maureen feel at ease.

Maureen's face said she wasn't convinced, but she dutifully sat down in front of the laptop I indicated.

"It's so easy. You use this touch pen," I showed her. "Can you just read that front page for me?"

I sat George at a laptop next to Maureen and asked him to do the same. "I'll just put your details on our quota sheet and I'll be back in a jiffie," I assured them.

As I returned, I managed to stifle my laughter. Both sat bent forward, eyes squinting to read the front page word for word. They weren't going to miss anything out in case their lives depended on it. There could be questions later!

"OK." I smiled broadly at them both. "If you've managed to read that can you press the continue bar at the bottom of the page."

The continue bar was coloured bright blue so as not to be missed.

Glancing at Maureen, she was so intent on reading each word, each syllable she remained bent almost double in an effort not to miss anything, her ample bosoms resting on the tabletop.

I gave it a few more minutes before asking again, "If you've finished reading could you touch the continue bar with the touch pen."

No response from either George or Maureen.

"Have you read the page?" I asked Maureen first.

"Page?" Maureen looked round.

"Yes, darling have you read the page?"

"You haven't given me a book," Maureen answered sincerely.

"Sorry, Maureen, have you read this screen?"

"Oh yes, dear. I've read that."

"Can you touch that continue bar at the bottom of the page, I mean screen?" I corrected myself.

Maureen looked back at the laptop. "Continue bar?" she queried.

"The 'continue' bar, yes," I said stretching out to touch the bar for her, "the big blue bar there with 'continue' written on it."

To be fair she wasn't on her own. Several people who never used a computer had missed it the first couple of questions.

"Oh, I see dear," she smiled

"George if you could do the same." I leaned towards George who seemed equally thrown by instruction of 'Continue Bar'.

"Oh yes I see now," he beamed back at me.

"These are just some of the questions I asked you outside," I said making note of what we call the respondent number which was at the top of the screen. "'Do you or any member of your household work in any of the following?' You said none of these. It's right at the bottom of the screen. If you can touch the 'none of these' button at the bottom of the screen, we can move on." George and Maureen studied the screen for what seemed like eternity.

"It's just there." I said again leaning forward to help them on their way.

"Oh yes, dear," George realised as I touched the relevant elusive answer to the first question.

"And now if you could touch the continue bar."

Again, a monumental pause.

"If you could touch the continue bar," I repeated.

George and Maureen seemed to be set in stone.

"If you could touch the 'continue' bar...." Again I leaned forward to point out the blue bar at the foot of the page, screen

"Right you are." George was picking it up in no time, Maureen was however a different kettle of fish. Not for love nor money could I get Maureen to focus. Her eyes were scanning the whole of the laptop in an endeavour to please me.

"There it is, Maureen, just at the bottom of the screen," I explained again.

"You said you lived in the Anglia region. That's right at the top. I said already leaning over Maureen to point out the location of the word "Anglia".

George had no trouble with this question. He had already touched Anglia, then sat back pleased with his efforts.

"Now the 'continue' bar," I added.

Still no response.

"Now if you could just touch the 'continue' bar," I said in my kindest voice.

The pauses began to resemble the mood on Remembrance Day, but with at least a ten minute silence in between each question.

"This one here dear?" George asked correctly.

"Yes, George." I said delighted at our progress.

Glancing over to check Maureen was following in his footsteps, I saw that she was once again scouring the laptop for the elusive continue bar.

"It's just there," I said touching the appropriate bar. The page turned over. "Now if you could just type in your age using the number keys." I pointed to the correct area where the number keys were on the keyboard.

George and Maureen both leaned over the laptops to check where I was pointing, then sitting back in their chairs waited patiently for further instructions.

"If you could just type in your ages," I asked again.

George and Maureen leaned over, checked the laptop, then both sat back as if they had been training with the Tiller Girls. Their timing was that impeccable.

"If you could just type in your age," I began again. "George, you're sixty three." I said pointing to the appropriate keys. "And Maureen, you're fifty nine."

"Yes, that's correct," George agreed but without making a move to type his information in.

"If you could type those numbers in," I said trying not to lose the plot myself.

George picked up on what he had been commanded to do and dutifully typed in fifty nine.

"No, you're sixty three." I politely corrected his mistake.

"So I am." He smiled, please that I knew his age.

"And Maureen, you're fifty nine," I said again pointing to the keys marked with those numbers.

"Yes, I am dear." Maureen uttered back at me.

"Yes, you're fifty nine. Just press that key there, number five, then that key there, number nine." I pointed again.

Maureen folded her arms over her rounded tummy, making sure her glance did not move from the screen, but made no move towards the laptop.

"If you could press that key, then that one, Maureen to put in your age," I said bobbing down to be at eye level with Maureen.

"Yes dear."

Still no movement.

"So it's that one," I said pressing the five, "then number nine. There. Your age is in."

"Good." Maureen sounded genuinely please with what we had achieved.

"Now on the next screen. It's asking you do you have any children in the household aged eighteen or under." My silent guess was no, but I tried to remain impartial.

No movement or sound from George or Maureen.

"Do you have any kids?" I simplified the question.

"Sorry, dear. You talking to me?" George asked.

"Um yes, George," I said, still squatting between them, wondering who else he had thought I was talking too. "Do you have any kids?"

"No dear, never lucky enough to have been blessed with them," George smiled.

Luckily for mankind, I unkindly thought. *A world with a miniature George and Maureen in really would have been a laugh a minute.* Then I made a mental apology to them both for thinking so harshly.

"So it's no then," I said pointing to the "no" button on the screen.

"No then," George agreed stretching forward to push said button.

"Same for you Maureen. You don't have any children," I smiled.

Maureen look shocked that I should know such a personnal details about her.

After more hesitation, I finally got her to touch the appropriate button.

"Now it's our old friend the 'continue' button. See this one," I said already touching the bar on Maureen's screen.

George obviously was feeling more confident. He removed his fixed glare from his screen to Maureen's to enable him to follow what I was doing, and then copied.

"So the next question is, 'Are you responsible for doing the grocery shopping?'" They were getting the swing of it now, well George was anyway.

"I like The Co-op," Maureen said still with her glare on the screen.

"Yes, so do I," I lied. "Do you do the grocery shopping Maureen?"

"Well depends if you can find one that's open," Maureen answered.

"What's open?" I foolishly asked.

"A Co-op," Maureen said flatly.

"Yeah," I agreed, but I was now loosing the will to live. "How about you, George, do you do the grocery shopping?"

"Cos they've closed so many of them," Maureen said before George could make that lifesaving decision. "Round our way they've closed the Co-op bank, as well as the village store. Bad enough when our post office went, now we has to come to Norwich for what's we need."

I wanted to hug Maureen. She had joined in on a conversation. It was lovely to hear her have an opinion on something.

"Yes," Maureen continued. "It's a long way on the bus from Wymondham."

My Auntie Jackie lives in Wymondham, although I don't use the local transport when I visit her each month. I know that Wymondham is, at the most, fifteen minutes in a car, approximately ten miles outside Norwich. Now I know I have the good fortune to have my own transport, but now found myself wondering if George or Maureen had ever been further than Norwich in their entire lives.

"So back to the survey," I tried again. "Do you do the shopping or do you go together?"

"Well depends," Maureen raised her gaze from the screen for the first time. "If there was a Co-op in the village I'd sometimes go down the road myself."

"But the Co-op's shut, isn't it?"

"Yes…"

"Right, so you both come to Norwich together to get the shopping." I was not sticking to the market research conduct any more. I shouldn't be deferring from the script, or putting words in the respondent's months.

"Yes." Again there was a look of amazement on Maureen's face, at how much knowledge I had at my fingertips about her and George's life.

"So it's this button here," I stretched forward again. "You do the shopping half the time."

"Well no." George stopped me. "We do all the shopping."

"Yeah, George that's not what it means. If you come into town together and buy the food together, that means you do it half or more than half the time." Before he could argue with me further I leant forward and touched the same button I had on Maureen's screen.

"Oh, I see," George nodded his head in agreement, but I don't think he really agreed with me. He was just being polite.

"Right, now I'm going to leave you to complete the rest of the survey by yourselves, on this new screen. You'll see lots of different questions all you have to do it read the question and put in a 'yes' or 'no' answer by touching the 'yes' or 'no' button. If you make a mistake," I pointed to the first question on Georges screen, "you can change it just by touching the other button." I touched the "no" button then the "yes" to demonstrate what I meant.

"Oh I see." George looked on in wonder at this technology.

Maureen said nothing.

"Thanks every so much for agreeing to take part. Hope you enjoy the survey." With that I turned leaving them to it.

After ten minutes I was lucky enough to find another kind soul who agreed to complete a survey. As we went up those six flights of stairs I asked the relevant questions: occupation of chief income earner, age, T.V. area she lived in, etc. I discovered my newest respondent was retired, aged sixty seven. She lived in East Anglia and was at the present time attending the local college doing a computer course. She went on to tell me that one of her grandchildren raced go-karts. He'd asked his Gran if she would join him at each circuit meet, to help sort out the necessary documents he needed. She had been involved in raising sponsorship for him through local businesses. Taking to the challenge, "like a duck to water," she raised over five thousand pounds of sponsorship in the first six months. She loved it.

"Just wish I'd took something like that up when I was young." she concluded as we reached the top of the stairs, me slightly out of breath, but not the remotest sign she was finding it hard going on the upwards climb.

I sat her down in front of the laptop away from George and Maureen and gave the briefest of explanations. Next thing I knew, she was ploughing on with the question without any need of assistance from me.

"You look as if you'll be fine. I'll leave you to carry on. If you do need any help just shout out. There's always one of us in the room to help," I said thanking her yet again.

"OK, love, you take care now," she smiled back.

"Excuse me dear." I heard George's voice call out.

"Yes, George. What can I do?" I looked down at his screen, which was still on the same page as I'd left him at ten minutes before, although he had filled in most of the answers with only a couple to go.

"I don't have a car that's four years old," he frowned.

"Oh, that's a shame. That means it won't let you do a survey," I lied. "Maybe you could do another survey for us on another day, George."

The page George had been stuck on for the last ten minutes was the page to determine which survey would be selected for him. At the rate he was going he would take up a laptop for the best part of the day. I looked over to Maureen's screen. She sat peacefully with her arms folded, just as I had left her, staring at the bright lights of the laptop. It was just beyond them both.

"Take your thank you note and pen my darlings, thank you so much for trying to help."

"That's alright, we likes to help if we can," George said helping Maureen to her feet.

"Well thank you so very much. It's a bit easier going down the stairs, Maureen," I smiled as they both turned at the doorway gave me a little wave goodbye and left.

"Were the hell you find them?" Mark my, colleague, who was minding the room asked. "Thick doesn't even cover it."

"Shut up, Mark. They were nice people. Just not very worldly," I hissed back

"Worldly. Don't think they were of this planet."

I looked over at my sixty seven year old respondent who was whizzing through her survey. Sixty seven and still active. She probably always would be. Then there was sweet Maureen and George. They wanted to help. They were kind enough even to try, knowing nothing of the technology placed before them. Picturing their faces as we had walked into the venue, the horror they must have felt at the prospect of having to use a laptop. It was totally alien to them, but they gave it their best shot. It wasn't that they were thick as Mark had said. It was just that they had lived in a different world.

The first time someone had mentioned 'cut then paste' to me when talking about a computer, I'd laughed saying, 'that was something I'd done as a child in a scrap book,' to cover my own lack of knowledge.

I am always grateful to those members of the public who are not rude to us as market researchers. Bonus if they have the time or inclination to take part in a survey, but the true beauty of this job is you meet so many different kinds of people.

Professional People Watcher

Before I did Market Research I would sometimes people watch. Sitting outside a café on a lazy summers day, watching people go about their busy lives, I would wonder what they did for a living, what was going on in their heads. Now I do it professionally. You have to have an eye for guessing their ages and what they do for a living. Believe me it's not always as straight forward as you would imagine.

Working in Ipswich during a bitterly cold winter day, our quota was to recruit only females, of different ages, to determine which facial creams they used.

We had nearly completed the quota, just the tail end left. I was hosting the venue, making cups of tea or coffee for any respondent that wished to have one. Pleased to be inside, instead of standing outside on that bitterly cold day. Looking up, a young colleague walked in with a middle aged man.

Now it will maybe sound crazy but sometime when you recruiting, it's easy to have a momentary lapse of memory, easy to forget maybe the approximate age of the respondents you are looking for, or for a solitary moment approach someone of the wrong gender. A male when you're looking for a female or vise-versa. I put these lapses down to having a senior moment. It does happen, but as I watched Susan walk in with this balding middle aged man complete with beer belly I couldn't hide the horror on my face.

Susan smiled back at me as if nothing was wrong. She sat the gentleman down at the laptop, checking to see if he wanted a cup of coffee or tea. Calmly, she walked over to the table where the quota sheet was to enter his details on it.

She'll realise now as she looks at the quota sheet what a silly-billy she's been. It's women only. No space for men on there, lovie.

But no, Susan completed the necessary details, walked sedately back to her gent and began the interview without a backwards glance.

"Susan," I quietly called over to her, "Susan can you come here for a moment."

"Excuse me for a moment." Susan got up and came over to me. "Yeah?" she asked.

"We're looking for females, you know girlies," I whispered to her.

"Yeah, I know," she shrugged.

"Females, not middle aged men," I whispered in her ear.

"Yeah, I know."

"That's a man." I felt stupid pointing it out.

"No that's a female," she grinned back.

I looked over to the chap, "That's no female, darling. That's a male."

Susan rolled her eyes, leaned forward and hissed, "That was once a female, but she's had the op, now she's a male, but on paper he's a 'she'."

The look of confusion on my face must have been apparent. "I'll explain later," Susan grinned, then she walked back to complete the survey with him – or was it her?

After thanking the respondent for completing the survey, Susan walked over to me to explain. "He was a 'she', but had the operation."

I still look dim, "How'd you mean."

"Well, she had a bit taken away and bits added," Susan laughed.

The penny finally dropped. She'd had a sex change. "Oh," I managed.

"But on paper," Susan explained as if talking to her extremely old, naive grandmother, "the law says you're still what you are when you're born. A girl is still a girl on their birth certificate. A boy is still a boy, so he is really a she."

"Are you sure that's true?" I questioned the reality of this ridiculous legislation.

"Yeah, my best friend's mum had the switch. Her name was Leslie but now her husband calls her Les. Lucky I guess she had a name that could swap over so easily," Susan said simply as if there was no problem.

"What do her kids call her?" I stupidly asked then wished I hadn't.

"Dad," Susan said without a flinch.

"Dad, oh yeah." This was far too complicated for my little brain.

Susan went back out into the street to find hopefully another female respondent. I was left trying to work out how families cope with this sort of complicated scenario. Wondering how you could still be a girl if you had gone through so much to become a boy. The titanic decisions you would have had to make. I decided I was lucky, enjoying being what I was born. I like being a female.

I Don't Want You To Be Afraid

I have been happily married to Peter for thirty plus years. He is my best friend. He makes me laugh and treats me like no one else can. I only have eyes for him, but I am human. I can still appreciate a handsome young man, or old one, come to that. My dad, who adored my mother, could sometimes be caught glancing at an attractive female. He would shrug it off by saying, "When I stop looking, put the lid on my coffin." I have seen Peter swiftly glance at a pretty girl. It's, I guess, human nature. So when you interview a nice chap, who is polite as well as charming, there is bound to be a bit of harmless flirting going on.

It was a lovely warm spring morning when I set off to work in Peterborough. I was looking forward to the day ahead. The Peterborough venue is lovely, one of my favourites. It's set close to the Cathedral. The staff working there are always so kind to us, spoiling us by making fresh coffee and providing us with the best homemade biscuits, which we would all pile into as soon as we arrive.

As I drove to Peterborough I thought how lovely it was to drive there during daylight after the long winter months when I left home in darkness and returned as dusk was falling. The blossom-filled trees lined the road. The day had a feel good factor already. I looked at my coat thrown over the passenger seat.

Don't think I'll need that today.

Arriving at the venue in good time, two other interviewers were already settled, tucking into the homemade short bread while sipping the piping hot coffee.

Lucy spoke first. "Lovely morning isn't it."

"Yes," I agreed.

"Coffee, Shelley?" I heard a voice say.

"Yes please, Sylvia." I turned, smiling.

"How have you been?" Sylvia enquired. "Haven't seen you for a while."

"Oh, I'm fine. You OK?"

We chatted about this and that, catching up on each other's family news as we munched the delicious biscuits. Then Dawn arrived, joining in with her recent news of a new baby granddaughter. Last but not least, Linda arrived, the other person in our team for the day. We briefly discussed the quota, then armed with our clip boards plus identification cards, went out into the bright sunshine to begin recruiting.

I was the youngest of the team. Sylvia was aged about sixty three, but looked more like fifty. Dawn was approaching her sixtieth birthday. Lucy and Linda I guessed, were about a couple of years older than myself. They were all in "good nick" or as Alfie would have said in the film of the same name, "In lovely condition."

By eleven we had already completed half the quota. An early finish was in sight. I was looking forward to lunch time as I always enjoyed working with this particular team. They were fun to work with. You could have a bit of a giggle with all of them. Maybe as we were the same generation give or take a bit, we all had similar back grounds and interests.

"Good morning, sir," I stopped a fellow of about forty five. "We're conducting market research would you be willing to take part in a survey."

"On what?"

"Oh it's just getting your opinions on different products and services." I beamed my best smile.

"Go on then," he smiled back.

As I walked with him towards the venue, I checked the other details I needed, making small talk as we walked along.

After seating him in front of the laptop I made him a cup of coffee. I made sure he fully understood what was required to complete the survey, thanked him again, and picked up my clip board to go outside.

As I opened the door, there stood Dawn, smiling from ear to ear. It was clearly apparent why. Standing next to her was, God's Gift to Women. He was tall, dark, and handsome with a smile that made you want to say, "Yes Please." His eyes were just so perfect, with a hint of naughty sparkle.

"Let me get that for you," he offered, in a voice that would soothe a storm at sea, as his strong arm pushed open the door to allow me to slip past him.

"Thank you," I said in a gentle girlie voice.

"It's just through there to the right, sir," I heard Dawn say in the sweetest voice imaginable.

"Do you want a cup of coffee or tea, sir?" I said now finding myself back in the venue not knowing how or why I'd slipped back in.

"That would be lovely," he smiled back.

"Which would you prefer, tea or coffee?" I almost purred.

"Tea would be great, thank you," came back his dulcet tones.

"Do you take sugar and milk?" I was now gazing into those clear blue eyes.

"Just milk, thanks," he smiled again.

Dawn shot me a glance. I shrugged my shoulders.

As I made the tea with the greatest of loving care, Dawn came up to me. "I would have made that," she hissed, although she was grinning.

"Bet you would," I laughed back at her.

"Do you want me to take his tea over to him?" I heard Lucy's voice.

"Or me," Linda and Sylvia echoed together.

"What are you lot doing in here?" Dawn asked.

"Same as Shelley. We came in to see if you need any help with him," Lucy giggled.

We all stood there smirking like fifteen year olds. Linda even had one leg bent with her foot on the wall, a silly grin of pleasure covering her face.

"What does he do for a living?" Sylvia asked

"Fireman, thirty seven, married but no kids," Dawn said pre empting our next questions.

"Fireman," Sylvia glowed.

"You lot can go out. I found him so I'll take his tea over, thank you Shelley," Dawn said taking the tea from my hand.

Once outside, the laughter must have been heard in Liverpool.

"He is a bit on the perfect side," Linda smiled, "but not in a big headed way".

"Polite too," I offered.

Without a cue from anywhere, we all began singing the Coca-Cola advert. "I don't want you to be afraid. I don't what you...." More giggles from all of us.

Twenty minutes later, after we had all nearly broken our necks recruiting to get back into the venue if only to get a glimpse of him again, offering him more tea than an elephant could have consumed, he had finished his survey.

"Thank you ladies," he said as he left.

"No, thank you," Linda said in a Marilyn Monroe voice. "We're *very* grateful."

"Grateful don't cover it," I whispered to Lucy.

We all watched as he strode off down the street. All of us were looking at his neat bum.

"He was so nice," Linda said not taking her eyes off him. "Don't think he knows just how lovely he is."

"And so lovely to look at," Lucy dribbled.

"Oh well, back to work," Sylvia sighed.

Half an hour later, we had nearly finished recruiting. Only two more respondents to go.

"He's back," Lucy shouted.

We all turned. Yes: there he was walking towards us, waving. We now all had our backs to the road, standing on the pedestrian walkway.

There was now a line of four middle-aged women, all clutching clipboards, smiling our sexiest smiles, waving franticly at this adorable creature, our eyes twinkling. He was walking straight towards us. It was only as he was almost level with us, that I caught a glimpse of the fire engine parked on the road.

Giggles overtook me. He wasn't waving at us but at his colleagues in the fire engine. What on earth must he have been thinking? Us all hell bent on waving at him, each of us with a fantasy that he was waving in our direction only. I caught sight of Linda out of the corner of my eye, her finger twisting round a strand of hair, her head tilted to one side. Lucy had a definite pout about her lips. Dawn was clearly breathing in. I was doing all of the above and then some.

He smiled as he walked pass us to join his fellow fire fighters. It was true what Linda had said. He wasn't one of those good looking guys who played on their looks, just a really nice fellow. Maybe he thought we were just thoughtful ladies, but my money's on him knowing that we'd all had an "mmm" moment.

It'll Be Alright On The Night

Over the years Peter and I have sometimes watched those programmes on the telly with various television or film celebrities offering up the bloomers that have happened while filming. We have often laughed out loud as some famous person loses the plot either by forgetting their lines, or are distracted by a plane going over head while filming a news documentary, or sometimes simply when a prop such as a door won't open, or a handle comes off in their hands. It is to the celebrity's credit that they allow these clips to be shown, giving us mere mortals a glimpse of their human frailties.

Working as a market researcher, I have found that similar things happen to all of us as happen to those brave celebrities shown on these types of programmes.

As most city centres are now covered by CCTV, I'm guessing that some of our bloomers are also captured on film, but as we aren't famous these will never been shown to the general public on T.V. but they can be just as funny.

The most common one is the fluffing of our lines. Everyone approaches the public in their own way, but with each of us it generally is the same sort of sentence.

I have my way, but there are those times when I say it wrong.

"Excuse me, market research conducting," Has been known to pass through my lips, only for me to smile sweetly at the understanding person I have just stopped, apologise, say something like "It's been a long day" and then force the correct spiel to come out.

There are, of course the slipping on a banana skin episodes. Walking along, clip board in hand, without warning you trip on an un-level pavement slab. One that you knew was there because you've seen it a hundred times before. For some unexplained reason you forget and over you go, picking yourself up as quickly as possible to scurry away to check your grazed knee, praying that no one has noticed, only to be stopped as you hobble off by a darling old lady who is perfectly sound on her pins as she asks if you're OK. Then you realise that the whole street of people has stopped to watch.

The summer had finally arrived. No more winter coats and yards of woollen scarves wrapped round your neck to keep out the biting wind. No more dripping wet umbrella or sexy thermal underwear. The sun was out to play.

Caution can now be thrown to the wind, I thought as I prepared to get ready for work.

I was wearing a floral summer frock with a light linen jacket along with new sandals which I'd bought in the sale just as last summer ended. They had a small heel but they were comfortable and smart enough to wear for work. I glanced out of the bedroom window. The bright yellow sun declared itself in a clear blue sky. It just gave you that feel good factor.

Once at work we all commented on what a lovely day it was, all of us looking as if we'd dressed for a Sunday School outing.

After the briefing on the type of survey we would be conducting, we all walked down the six flights of stair from the venue room with a defiant skip in our step, out into the warm summer day.

"New shoes, Shelley?" Jane asked,

"Yeah, lovely to have the toes out on show," I smiled back at Jane.

"Makes a change from being all bundled up, doesn't it?" she beamed back.

"Sure does."

The morning went well. Sunshine seemed to make the members of the public more willing to stop, listen to you spiel and then take part in the survey. A bit of sunshine cheers everyone up.

We had to find some youngsters, sixteen to eighteen year olds, preferably female. I spied two girls walking towards me.

"Excuse me girls, could you help us with a survey?" I asked as they got level with me.

"Go on then," the pretty young blonde one said.

"Can I just check you ages?" I smiled back at them.

"Sixteen," they both said together.

"Great. You're just the right age we're looking for. We're conducting the surveys in that building over there." I pointed towards the venue.

They followed me as I asked the remaining questions relevant to the screening to check they were suitable to do the survey. They fitted perfectly.

As I opened the door, I explained there were a lot of stairs as we were working on the top floor. They said that was fine. Leading the way I lifted my foot to take the first step and misjudged it completely, somehow managing to land on the edge of the step above. The next few seconds felt like an eternity. My right foot rung over, my other foot somehow trying to help by doing nothing. My body was now unsure of what it was going to do. My hand reached out for the banister but again I misjudge the distance, my hand falling inches short of the damn thing. I was falling as gracefully as I could and before I knew it, I lay spread over the top six steps. I heard a thud – or was it the breath being thumped out of me as I landed? – and, then the tiny clatter of my clip board as it fell from my hand to the bottom of the stairs where the two young girls stood.

"Are you OK?" the blonde asked.

I wanted to say, "What do you think?" but instead as ever the true professional that I am, I staggered gracefully, to my feet, ignoring the burning pain that had suddenly broken throughout my entire body. "No No I'm fine," I muttered as I bent down to collect my clip board plus sandal which had fallen from my dainty foot during the commotion.

"Looks like it's broken," declared the other youngster as we all looked down at the sandal.

"Yes," I agreed with her looking at the ripped strap. "Well it's just up here." I thought I'd better carry on, for some reason making a split second judgement that there was no time to take the other sandal off. So, with my clip board and broken sandal in one hand and the other firmly placed on the banister, just in case I faltered, we began the long climb.

I don't really blame them, but half way up the stairs I heard the first snuffled giggle as they followed me up the six flights of stairs. In truth I'd have been laying on the floor in stitches having just witnessed such a spectacular fall, then having to follow this crazy women as she limped, half through the pain, emphasized more by the fact that she hadn't removed her other shoe. Why I hadn't done this still remains a mystery to this day.

By the time we reached the top floor, they couldn't contain themselves any longer. They were holding they're sides, snorting, tears running down their faces. I tried not to make eye contact. Sitting them in front of the laptops, I briefly explained what was expected of them. How much they took in of what I was saying is hard to say as I couldn't hear myself over the now unleashed laughter that they had given into.

I limped over to the table where the quota sheet lay.

"They seem happy." Alan stated the obvious.

"Hmm," I agreed.

"Why are you holding your shoe Shelley?" he asked.

"Well they're new," I explained, as if that was all I needed to say.

We also have our own props, which can cause problems.

One time, I had been given a job of what we call "Capi Door to Door". This involves visiting people's houses and conducting the interview in their homes on a laptop. Some interviewers hate this type of work, but I really enjoy it. I find it relaxing – well, most of the time! This particular job was also a placement. It involved a short interview then the depositing of the product, in this case chocolate biscuits, with the respondent calling back to see what they thought of it a week later. Nothing could be easier.

I had charged the laptop the night before and gone through the necessary paperwork. I left home confident of the day ahead.

I drove to a local housing estate, sure that I would find the right types of people I needed to complete my quota. Parking the car in a quiet cul-de-sac I grabbed the case with the laptop in, plus the necessary paperwork to being my door knocking.

It was to be my lucky day. The first door I tried was a "yes". I walked into this dear old chap's home explaining that I was just going to ask a few questions. These would be recorded on the laptop. Then I would leave him with the chocolate biscuits, explaining that, depending on the public's reaction to them, they would either be marketed or not. He seemed thrilled to be taking part in such an event.

"It's all clever stuff," he stated, staring at the bright lights of the laptop as the first screen opened up.

"Yes, it all gets recorded on here, then tonight I send it all back down the telephone line," I explained.

"Marvellous," he beamed.

He was a little darling. Although he was seventy four, he was bright as a button, fully understanding each part of the survey. There was no need to prompt him. He was answering the questions without hesitation. He told me his wife had passed away two years ago. They had been married for forty two years, happily married he added. They had two sons. He was just charming company.

"Now my darling if you wouldn't mind just signing this. It tells you what ingredients are in the biscuits." I handed him the disclaimer which goes with every trial placement.

"And your coming back in a week to see what I think after I've tried them?" he looked over the top of his glasses as he signed the paper I'd handed him.

"Yes we said 10 O'clock next Friday, if that OK?"

"Fine. I'll look forward to it." His eyes twinkled.

I was now fumbling in my bag. No biscuits. I'd remembered the laptop, paperwork, etc, but had left the biscuits at home.

"Oh, I'm so sorry." I sighed. "I'll have to pop back. I'd forget my head if it wasn't screwed on. I've left the biscuits at my home. I'm so sorry."

"Don't worry. I'll be here. You take your time." He smiled.

"I'll be back before you know it," I said as I left him standing in the doorway.

"You drive carefully, no rush," he said waving me goodbye.

I was so cross at myself.

How could I have been so stupid as to forget the product?

Throwing the things into the car I keep thinking I was going to lose at least an hour by the time I'd drove home got the product and driven back, what an idiot.

As I pulled out of the cul-de-sac I was ready to put my foot down, having never been a slow driver.

At least some of the trip back was on the by-pass, so I could maybe make a bit of time up there. Turning the first corner, my accelerator foot at the ready, my hopes of a speedy journey were dashed. Sitting at the traffic lights was Mr & Mrs Plod in their bright shiny police car. Having driven for twenty years or more, I have so far only ever got three points on my licence, having deserved far more. Also, doing the miles with this job, you need your transport as you never know where you will be working. There was no way I was going to risk getting more points. I muttered under my breath as I pulled up extremely sedately behind the police car. The lights turned green,

There is a God.

He turned left and I was going right.

Now slowly does it, till he's out of sight, then into warp speed.

I watched carefully in my rear view mirror. It was clear. Then I heard the siren. Being a law abiding citizen, I pulled over to allow whatever emergency service the space it needed to overtake me. Sitting quietly beside the road I glanced in my rear view mirror only to see it was Mr & Mrs Plod, lights ablaze, coming my way. I waited for them to overtake. The siren seemed very loud. Then I realised they had pulled up behind me. Mrs Plod got out of the car.

Why is it that when you're confronted by a police officer your face automatically goes ripe like a red tomato? I gingerly wound down the window.

"Can I help you, officer?" I smiled weakly, sure that my bright red face must be dazzling her.

"Did you want this?" she asked as she reached up to the roof of my car, pulling the laptop from the roof.

"Oh my God, thank you, thank you so much." I flushed even brighter if that were possible.

"That's OK." She smiled as she turned to go back joining her colleague who was sat shaking his head at the stupid women who had drove off from somewhere with her laptop on the roof.

"Thank you again," I called after her.

I guess I'd been in such a rush to get the biscuits, I'd plonked the laptop on the roof, thrown the other bits and bobs in the car, then in my haste just driven off.

The moral, as with those film and television celebrities, is: always beware of your props.

Guess Who I Met Today.

You never know who you're going to meet doing market research. That's part of what makes this job such an adventure. But sometimes it's a bit scary.

Peter was concerned when I first began the job. "What about all the whakos? What if you meet someone who's a bit odd?"

I reassured him I would be alright, but in truth it can be a bit of a risk, especially when you're going into someone's house. You have to rely on your instincts to a certain degree, but even then people can turn out to be something other than they first seemed, as a colleague of mine found out.

Clare had been conducting a door to door survey on, of all things, wallpaper. She related this tale to me some months after I started working in my new found career. She didn't tell me to frighten me, but to make sure I was aware of the possible dangers.

She was working in a perfectly respectable neighbourhood. Her day had gone well. At the next house she called at she was invited in by a "lovely couple". They were more than happy to discuss wallpaper and decorating as they had recently renovated several rooms in the house, including the bathroom, which now had a beautiful corner bath complete with all fixtures and fittings. The couple insisted that Clare take a look at their pride and joy, the sumptuous bathroom. Clare stood in the doorway of the bathroom admiring the colour scheme, while the husband stood close to his wife, his arm around her shoulder, explaining to Clare every detail of how they had worked together to get the finished effect. After completing the survey they asked Clare if she would like a cup of coffee or maybe even something to eat. Clare declined their kind invitation explaining she was picking her husband up from work in half an hour. As she left the house she remembered thinking what a happily married couple they seemed.

Only one week after calling on them Clare read in the local paper that he had been charged with murdering his wife, firstly by putting drugs in her coffee and then cutting her into little bits in the beautiful corner bath.

It makes you sit up and think.

Having said the above, you don't meet many bath murderers that are into wallpapering. Most people are your run of the mill sort, but the range is amazing.

On yet another door to door survey, this time about banks and building societies, a subject most people have a variety of opinions on, not all of it good if the truth be known, I was plodding my way round a small housing estate. I could see this elderly chap working in his garden. He looked up. I smiled as I approached him.

"Good afternoon Sir," I said, pulling my un-resistible market researcher's smile. "I'm conducting market research into people opinions about banks. Would you be willing to take part in a survey?"

"What's that you say?" came back the perfect Eaton-educated voice.

"I'm conducting market research…" but before I could finish, he cut me off.

"Well you'd jolly well better come in," he said, striding towards to the back door.

Before I could thank him for taking part, he was sitting at the kitchen table full of anticipation.

"Banks you say. Better get the old girl involved. She deals with all my finances." He turned and hollered, "Jean, Jean there's some young girl here wanting to ask us a few questions on banking."

I had to smile at the young girl bit. He looked to be around seventy five. His kind remark was extremely sweet and I secretly thanked him for it.

Jean appeared in the doorway dressed in a designer leisure suit complete with green tea cosy on her head.

How did I know she'd look like that?

"Richard, what are you shouting about?" Jean looked at him sternly.

"This young woman is doing some sort of survey on those banker types. Thought it might be a good idea to tell them what we think old girl."

"Richard I'm trying to sort out the charity auction for Saturday. Can't you do it." Jean was obviously stressed. Maybe due to the woollen tea cosy making her a little too warm.

"Well I'm no use. I don't deal with that sort of thing. Anyway I've said we'll do it now." Richard was disappointed Jean didn't share his enthusiasm for this new project.

"Very well Richard, but I must get on. Mrs Brown-Smyth is popping round in half an hour." Jean took her dutiful place beside her husband at the kitchen table.

"Thing is, I don't carry money around, can't see the point." Richard turned towards me obviously pleased Jean was there to support him.

"Well it's you I'd like to interview. Could I ask you name, it's Mr...."

"Wellington. That's W-E-L-L-I-N-G-T-O-N."

"Can I ask which of these you have an account with?" I showed Richard the card with a list of banks and building societies listed there.

"Lord, I don't know, do you Jean?" he half turned to Jean to enquire.

Jean bent forward to check the list causing her tea cosy to move slightly over her forehead.

"Richard, you do know it's this one." Jean gave me the answers I needed, listing several of the names of high street banks and building societies. It was obvious they had a few bob.

"And which of these do you have savings with?" I asked.

"All of them don't we?" Richard enquired of Jean.

The survey went on for about three quarters of an hour, with each question I asked, Richard would repeat the question for Jean's sake, occasionally arguing with her if he thought her answer wasn't correct, only to be told by Jean to shut up.

"Thank you very much for your time Mr and Mrs Wellington," I said handing them the thank you note and a couple of pens.

"It's Lord," Richard smiled taking the pens. "Thank you for these, very handy."

"Lord?" I questioned "Sorry I thought you said your name was Wellington."

"Yes 'tis," Richard said flatly.

"Wellington?" I repeated.

"Yes."

"Well thank you for your time again." I stood up to leave. "Lovely to have met you Mr Wellington, and you Mrs Wellington."

"It's Lord," Richard retorted.

"What he's trying to say," Jean interjected "is that he's a Lord, that Lord Wellington."

"Yes," said Richard as if everyone knew.

"Oh sorry, Lord Wellington." The penny dropped. "Well thank you Lord and Lady Wellington for your time." Then I wondered if I'd addressed them correctly.

"No need to curtsy me dear," Richard beamed.

"Right, thank you again."

As I left the house I had to smile, you just never know who you're going to meet in this job.

We are always supposed to probe when asking about the occupation of the of the chief income earner, to see if their responsible for any staff for example. This would change were a person would fit in a quota. If they are a skilled manual worker we should ask what sort of work they do. Someone people tell you they are an Engineer and once you've probed you may find that they are a Project Engineer with a degree, or at the other end of the spectrum, they could be a skilled sheet metal worker, which is entirely a different thing. Probing can backfire on you sometimes as my college Rachel found out to her embarrassment. After stopping a young woman in the street, Rachel asked what the occupation was of the chief income earner.

"A prostitute," the woman answered frankly.

Taken aback, Rachel then went on to ask, "Do you work with your hands?"

"Yes, love, and other bit too," came the cheeky reply.

I fell about laughing when Rachel told me about this incident. It can so easily happen if you probe too much, I guess.

Education Is A Wonderful Thing.

Education is truly a wonderful thing. While I was never the dimmest in my class, I was also far from being the brightest. To get my qualifications I always had a long hard slog of revision before any exam. I think I can hold my own when it comes to mixing with people from many different walks of life. I am able to converse in most subjects, but I am never going to be a scholar. However, I think I do possess common sense, being able to pick up most things fairly quickly. I didn't go on to university, but maybe one day I'll do an Open University course. Who knows? Sometimes in my job I meet highly educated folk, with not a grain of common sense. My very dear friend Susan went on to become a teacher. We have been friends for so many years.

Once she confided in me, "You know Shelley, I have never really left school."

"How'd you mean Susan?" I asked.

"Well think about it," she went on. "I left school, went to uni, and then went back to school to teach. See – never really left school. Never been out in the big wide world. I guess you could say I've been in the Education System forever, a bit institutionalised."

I'd never thought about it like that, but she had a point, which brings me to my next story.

I was offered a large contract in Cambridge, "The Seat of Leaning," for a government department. The job entailed visiting pre selected addresses to find out how people in Cambridge got from one place to another. The interviews were very short, but if the respondent was happy to take part in a further part of the survey, I was to ask them if they would keep a diary on their movements for the following week, calling back to collect said diary. They in turn would receive a

£5 voucher to spend in various high street stores. The job, unlike any other market research job I had encountered, had a massive amount of paperwork with it, so, armed with a brief case and my ever-so-posh clip board, I set off to visit the streets of Cambridge.

I said a silent pray of thanks to my SatNav as I pulled up on one of the streets of pre selected addresses. I would never have found it in such a short time without Drew-cilla – my nickname for my SatNav. We had a strange working relationship Drew-cilla and I. Often I would curse her thinking she had sent me in the wrong direction, only to find out she had not. She was always polite even when she instructed me to 'turn around when possible' if I took a wrong turn.

Checking the door numbers I trundled along until I found the correct address. I had found that most people were happy to take part in the survey, given the subject. More than seventy percent of the addresses I visited turned out to have respondents with PhDs or Masters, most of them having a higher educational qualification of some sort.

Knocking on the door, I could hear the sound of a running shower coming from an open window in one of the upstairs rooms. Then heard a woman's voice shout out

"Get that, Bob, or Cindy will you."

I waited patiently. Neither Bob nor Cindy answered the door, making me think that maybe they'd not heard their instruction. As I had so many visits to complete in a day I decided to go to the next address on my list for that street.

At the next address the lady who answered the door was from America, working here as a teacher. She was pleasant enough and we completed the survey in less than ten minutes. She declined the diary.

I called back at the address where I'd heard the shower running, knocking on the door for the second time.

"Who's there?" a voice called out from the upstairs room with the open window.

"Hello," I shouted towards the window, "I'm conducting market research…."

"What?" her head peered out of the window.

"We're conducting market research for a government department at selected address, one of them being yours…"

"Hang on," she shouted back at me.

It didn't take long before she answered the door, holding it open just enough so I could see half of her face.

"What was that you were saying?"

I explained it all again.

"Oh," she grunted. "Well you better come in." She opened the door very slightly allowing me to squeeze through.

"Thank you," I said, trying to show her my ID before entering the house, having some difficulty given the size of the gap of the opening.

"That's OK," she glanced at my ID. "Got to keep the cats in. Back you go, Bob. You too, Cindy," she said ushering two cats with her foot to the stairwell.

Warning bells should have gone off then. Only twenty minutes ago, had I not heard her telling Bob or Cindy to get the door.

Think logically Shelley. Then again, maybe it was to let callers know she was not alone in the house. Hold that thought.

The house was clean and tidy. Lots of books were stacked neatly on shelves surrounding the room. The odd water colour here and there adorned the walls.

"Who's the artist?" I asked trying to break the ice.

"Me." That was all she said.

I quickly ran through why I was there, after which she said she would be more than happy to take part in the survey. I mentioned that it should only take ten minutes, tops.

Running quickly through the demographic questions she informed me that she had two Masters Degrees: one in physics, the other in Native American art.

Things went OK until the third question. "How many hours do you spend walking in an average week?" I asked.

"Well, I don't," she said blandly.

"That's fine nil then," I said entering her answer onto the questionnaire.

"Well no that's not the reason," she interrupted me. "It's because of this bone here." She pointed to her thigh then moved her hand upwards towards her hip bone. "Can't any more, I just can't." She gazed off into space.

"So…" I began. "Do you walk anywhere?"

No reply was forthcoming. She was still in the room, but methinks away with the fairies. I tried again. Same question, but still nothing forthcoming. I decided to leave the first answer she'd given me as nil.

"How many hours do you spend cycling?" I asked.

"Ah," she began, "Now that's different."

"Good." I felt pleased we would be getting somewhere. "So how many?"

"Yes I do," she offered, a strange smile crossing her face.

"So roughly how many hours in a week do you cycle?"

"Yes," she smiled.

"That would be how many hours in a week?"

"Well that would depend."

"What would it depend on?"

"If one attended night school."

"So you attend night school? Is that each week in term time?" I was guessing she we thinking school hols would mean something different.

"No," she looked at me blankly.

"OK." I couldn't keep the sigh out of me voice. "So in an average week how many hours do you use your bicycle?"

"Yes I do," she answered, still unaware that murder might be done in that airy room. I would walk away from it. No one would know apart from Bob and Cindy, and I could rely on them to keep their mouths closed.

The rest of the interview was much the same. I learned that her gardener was now in prison, but didn't find out why. I learned that she couldn't reach the centre of her walled garden because of something he'd done, and of course, because of her bone – thigh and hip – which she stroked as she mentioned them again. She used to go to night school, but why she stopped will always remain a mystery. Maybe it was them bones again. Christ I had lost the will to live by question seven.

"I hate asking this question," I admitted, "but what is the total income of the household before deductions? By that I mean tax, or national insurance, that is your gross income before these types of deductions?"

"Gross? What do you mean 'gross'?" she enquired.

"Your income before any deduction," I asked plainly.

"Gross what is gross?" she stared at me as if I was the one from another planet.

"Your household income, before deductions, tax etc," I tried so hard.

Her hand reached out, pulling my questionnaire from my grasp.

"Gross, gross." she muttered as she circled the word on the questionnaire. "What do you mean by gross?"

I was too weather worn to even try and explain it again, but then, as if a light went on, she checked the various options on the questionaire, then circling a figure.

Without a moment to lose I pulled the questionnaire back off her.

"Thank you so much, that is the survey completed." My mind scurried over the possibility: Would she would want to take part in a week's worth of diary, meaning I'd have to call back. I would be consumed by guilt at not offering, so I asked the fatal question.

"Would you be willing to take part in a further survey by keeping a diary on your movements for the coming week?" I hoped, someone was facing Mecca, praying for me, praying that she would refuse. "You receive a £5 voucher as a small thank you for time."

"Oh that sounds like fun. £5 you say. Does one deposit in one's bank?" she asked coming to life at the thought of a fiver. Given the fact the figure she had circled for her income was ridiculously high, although we weren't sure if that was gross or not, a fiver seemed a tiny amount of money.

"No it's a 'Love to Spend Voucher'," I informed her.

"Oh," she said as if she understood. "Tell me do you know why on Clements Road they have a police cordon and tent there?" she asked.

Where that had popped from, I was unsure. One minute we were talking about the voucher, the next we were off down St Clements Road, with the Police involved.

"Sorry I'm not local," I informed her.

"So why do they have that cordoned off, would you say?" she asked again.

The fact that I didn't have a clue where Clements Road was in Cambridge didn't occur to her, so my reply was, "I think it because of McDonalds."

"Oh I see." She seemed happy with the answer.

I left the house, proud of myself. I had used such great self control. Murder had not been done. Maybe it had at Clements Road, but not in that house. Still, the nagging thought of a further visit in a week's time was depressing.

The following week the gods smiled down on me. Miss Away with the Fairies had left a "sort of" completed diary on the door step for me. I say "sort of" because she had crossed some of the wording out and written her own interpretation of the question. Then there were a couple of days when she had not completed it at all. Maybe she didn't go out – at least, that's what I think the lines struck across the pages meant. A neat hand-written note was also left, stating she had had to pop out for the day. It also asked that I deposit her £5 in her bank account. She had enclosed her building society branch address, as well as her account number and sort code to enable me to do so. I destroyed her note and posted her voucher through the door, thanking the gods for their countless blessings, thrilled that I did not have to struggle to explain that she could only use the voucher in the shops listed and that it was impossible to bank it.

Health & Hygiene

Surveys about personal health are always easy. Everyone seems as if they want to tell you all about their back troubles: diabetes, or whatever aliments they have. On the few times I have had to sit in a doctors or hospital waiting room there are always people happy to share details about their most intimate health problems with a perfect stranger. While I am happy just to sit there while trying to read the posters which adorn those otherwise boring corridors, reminding myself mentally to make an optician appointment, as I can never quite make out the smaller writing.

My friend and colleague, Anna, had to conduct a survey finding people suffering with athlete's foot, asking what remedy they found best for this condition. Anna confessed it was a delicate subject but she had managed to find most of her required quota. She was on the last leg of the job when she stopped a young man in his mid thirties who disclosed that he did indeed suffer from this condition. Anna invited him to sit on a nearby bench to conduct the interview. One of the questions involved showing him a list of creams that could be used to sooth the condition.

"Which of these do you use?" Anna asked showing him the long list of creams.

"This one, and this one, and, oh yes, that one," he answered, pointing to various makes.

"Which one do you find most soothing for your athletes foot?" Anna asked.

"None of them," he answered calmly.

"But you said you suffered from athletes foot?" Anna checked.

"Yes I do," he nodded, "but I don't use those creams for that."

"Oh what do you use them for?" Anna enquired.

"For the spots and sores round my privates." He answered truthfully, without flinching.

Anna terminated the interview then and there.

Most of the venues we work in are often on the second or third floor of a building, unless they have a lift which most of them don't. This makes it impossible to recruit anyone who is disabled. Market research companies try and cover this by sending interviewers out into the street to conduct interviews or by doing house to house so we can at least try and amend this situation. The only venue where it is possible to get a person in a wheel chair in is Peterborough, this being on the ground floor. However, this venue is tiny. Not enough room to swing a cat. You can get a wheel chair in there, but only just.

I was working with Jenny in Peterborough on a horrible rainy day, one of those when you question why you're doing this sort of job. Your mind wanders off. You begin fantasizing about a warm fire at home with a large mug of coco snuggled in your soft dressing gown – creature comforts at their best. Instead you lean against the wind trying to stop people walking through town. Obviously they think you're some sort of barm-cake standing out in that sort of weather, armed with a clip board and soaking wet recruitment sheet, your eye make-up dripping slowly down your face, and who can blame them? We must look a scary sight.

Jenny was not having a good day. She had only recruited two people. I wasn't much better, having only recruited three.

"Had better," Jenny announced

"Yeah, feel like packing in," I agreed. "Nearly 3 o'clock. Only another hour."

Jenny shrugged

I smiled back at her, noticing a couple heading towards her. The woman was what my Grandmother used to call 'nicely rounded'. Her plump little arms were holding onto the arm of her husband's motorised wheel chair. They stopped as Jenny spoke to them. Jenny nodded, smiled at them, and turned, taking them towards the venue.

The motorised wheelchair was somewhat large, a bit of a Rolls-Royce of wheelchairs.

It'll be a tight squeeze getting that type of wheelchair through the door, but hey maybe it'll go.

I asked the next passerby if they would take part in a survey

"You must be frozen. Go on then I'll help you out," said this kind soul.

Walking down to the venue and making small talk, I checked to see if they would like a cup of coffee or tea.

"Tea would be lovely," was the reply.

Once we got into the tiny venue, we were unaware of the bedlam that was about to take place. Jenny's lady respondent was sat working her way through a survey on the laptop while two other respondents were sat at the other laptops completing their surveys. The husband of Jenny's respondent was wedged in the middle of the room, stuck in his larger than life motorised wheel chair, with not enough room to turn it. He sat facing a blank wall.

"Let get you turned round," Jenny offered.

"That's alright luv, I can manage," he hollered back at Jenny, obviously thinking she was hard of hearing.

With that, he slammed the wheelchair into reverse, running over Jenny's foot causing her to yelp out in pain. Ever the professional, she continued on, hugging her poor foot with one hand while still grasping her clip board in the other.

"Let's get you..." she began.

"No I can manage," he screamed over his shoulder as he banged it into first, moving forward, hitting the blank wall he'd been staring at with enough force to demolish it.

I watched on in disbelief as he tried to do a three point turn, first turning slightly then crashing the wheelchair into a table which caused the laptop placed there to fall to the floor with a thud.

"Oh." was all he said as he cranked it back into reverse, moving into a tiny space between the other respondents, running over their neatly placed shopping bags on the floor.

"Sorry about that luv," he smiled weakly at her as she tried to recover her shopping from under his wheels. Without a second thought he clicked the gears into first again this time moving forward at a rate of knots any cruise ship would have been proud of, approaching the table upon which Jenny had replaced the laptop. Jenny jumped not a moment too soon as he hit the same table. We watched in stunned silence as the whole thing collapsed, sending the laptop hurtling to the floor, sparks coming from it followed by a weak smoke signal.

"Unplug it," Jenny screamed at me.

I moved forward, suddenly aware that he was now facing my direction. It was going to hit me: a full on collision. I remember letting out a small squeal as I jumped out of the way, landing in a heap on the floor, showing off to everyone in the room what a true athlete with natural poise and elegance I was. Now the opposite wall took his fancy. He charged towards it. I closed my eyes. Someone was going to get hurt.

I felt the crash go through my entire body.

"Sorry about that luv," he turned, having had to come to a standstill as he was now wedged between the table with all our paperwork on, the same table where we made the coffees. "Not had this thing long. Still learning how to work the contraption."

Jenny was now standing beside him. "Let me help you."

"No, luv I've got to master it." He was already throwing it into reverse.

I stood wondering which poor soul in the room was going to have to be accompanied to the local hospital, and how I would explain the injuries.

"Well there was this man in a motorised wheel chair..." *They just won't believe it.*

I glanced over to his wife, who seemed unaffected by the commotion. She went on watching the adverts and clicking her responses in with the touch pen. The other respondents however had all turned to watch the madness of the Demolition Derby.

I had now unplugged the smouldered laptop. Jenny had jumped clear of the wheel chair as it collected speed, heading for the wall at the back of the room. There was yet another crash as he hit the opposite side of the room, causing him to jolt somewhat in the seat.

Undeterred by this, he collected himself quickly and headed straight for Jenny and I.

I wanted to shout "Every man for himself," but thought it might not be appropriate. Instead I leapt out of the way with only a second to spare. Jenny stood motionless waiting for the impact.

I remember shouting her name as she fell to the floor, her clip board covering her face. All I could do was copy her and covered mine.

"Think I've finished," his wife announced.

As I opened my eyes I noticed she was now standing up, the wheel chair demon had stopped inches away from Jenny as she lay crouching on the floor awaiting her fate.

"You managed to get that thing turned round then," Mrs Wife smiled at hubby.

"Thank you," I heard my wobbly voice saying.

He punched the gears, now in full control, gliding forward, effortlessly rolling out the door, Mrs Wife walking behind him.

Jenny pulled herself up. "I saw my whole life flash before me." She gasped, brushing the coffee powder from her hair. It had fallen from the coffee table where she had taken up the recovery position in order to protect herself.

We looked round the room. Two chairs lay on the floor, one of the tables legs lay crushed from the blow it had received. A small dent in the far wall was proof that this had moments ago, been an unlikely war zone.

The laptop in my hand was still warm from the small fire which had flared over its circuits. Plastic coffee cups lay empty on the floor near Jenny's feet, the dark coloured power still apparent in her hair. Papers from the other table covered the floor.

I looked over at Jenny. She was still in shock, but the bubbles of laughter now took over. I couldn't contain them.

"It's not funny," Jenny stressed.

"No it's not," I struggled to get out, before the laughter took over.

"How are we going to explain the laptop?" Jenny frowned.

I got control for a moment. "Well we'll just tell them there was this man in a wheel chair." That was all I could manage.

Fun Making Up

We can all cause embarrassment to those we love. I remember as a teenager thinking my parents were the most embarrassing people to walk the planet. My mum was such a colourful person. Her style of dress ranged from bright pink to even brighter pink. Her choice of hats resembled those of the character of Hoss, played by Dan Blocker in *Bonanza*, a sort of huge domed effort placed on her head in bright shades, full blown colours of pink, red or even yellow. I recall cowering on the school bus floor knowing that she had decided, as a surprise to come and collect me herself. I prayed as I hid there that she would not enter the bus and call my name, which of course she always did. Dad on the other hand was a little more subdued but even he could make me flush a deep shade of red by insisting he wanted to collect me safely after my night at a local disco. I'll never forget him standing there in collar and tie, but with his slippers still on.

I too have embarrassed my kids in only a way a mother knows how. They have many stories to tell.

Peter has this annoying habit of making a hissing sound when concentrating. He's totally unaware he is doing it. He hisses while out shopping, as he tries to decide which purchase he will make, oblivious to the shop assistant waiting patiently. He'll just stand there, hissing away to himself like a kettle coming to the boil. I have mentioned this to him on several occasions but he is so unaware of it, I think he thinks I'm making it up.

When interviewing you can sometimes recruit a couple, and while one of them is more than happy to take part, the other will be angry that their partner or spouse has made them stop to take part in a survey. They could be getting on with whatever they have come to town to do. Sometimes the one that didn't want to join in will start to interject, putting their own opinion forth, but as you can only take the answers of the person you have recruited. It can all get a bit confusing to everyone concerned. There are the times when you recruit a person seeming to be on their tod, then along comes the partner, wanting to know why they didn't turn up at the arranged meeting point, only to be told they got stopped by this market researcher. They place the blame fully on your shoulders, so you are the one that gets the sideways glances at this rude interruption to their day out.

There have been several times when I have stopped couples only to find that they are both more than willing to help. On some surveys you can take two or more people from a household, but the rule of thumb is usually only one.

This can cause more problems than you can imagine, not only does it take the couple more time to decide whom is going to take part than it would do to do three surveys, you also have to deal with the rejected one feeling left out. Or the discussion of who is going to do the survey can turn into a domestic incident. On one such occasion this was to be, to my cost.

Working in Norwich on a beautiful hot summer day, people seemed happy to be out, just taking time to have a look round, generally enjoying soaking up the sunshine.

"Excuse me sir, madam. We're conducting a survey about shopping habits. Would one of you like to take part?" I began my spiel.

"Shall we?" The woman asked her partner.

"Yeah if you want," he smiled back at her.

"Which one of you would like to take part?" I asked

"You do it," she said, gazing up at him

They were obviously head over heels with each other.

"No you can do it."

"Oh I don't mind. You do it," she beamed back.

"Would you like to do the survey?" I directed my glance toward him.

"I don't mind, Cathy can do it," he said without removing his stare from her.

"No, John, you do it." She wrinkled her pretty little nose at him.

"Would you like to do it?" I moved my eyes to try make contact with her, but they were having none of it. They only had eyes for each other.

"You do it." His voice was a bit firmer now.

"OK I'll do it." She giggled.

Walking them towards the venue I discovered that they had only just married two weeks previously, and had just returned from honeymoon in Jamaica. They even managed to hold hands walking up the narrow stair case without taking their eyes off each other.

"Would you like a cup of coffee or tea?" I asked as we entered the venue.

"That would be lovely," she answered.

"Not for me," he said

"I won't have one then."

"You have if you want to." He looked back at her.

"Not if you're not going to," she pouted.

Lovely as all of this was, they were beginning to get on my nerves a little. I tried to think back to when Peter and I had begun our married life. We hadn't been able to afford a honeymoon after paying the deposit on our tiny rented flat, but had both taken a week off work to get the flat into some sort of shape.

A smile passed my lips as I remembered decorating the small but cosy living room in deep purple, thinking it would be the fabulous, most beautiful sitting room ever. Peter was amazed that I could spread so much paint over so many surfaces other than the walls. Every part of my clothing ended up stained with paint and my hair looked as if it had had a purple rinse.

"God Shelley, could you have got it anywhere else?" Peter had smiled as he gingerly took the sticky paint brush from me.

"Yeah," I said as I kissed him spreading paint over his face as I did so.

We didn't finish decorating that tiny living room for the rest of the week.

Maybe we were as daft as these two once.

"So would you like tea or coffee?" I tried again

"No that's alright, if John doesn't want one, I'll be OK." She answered.

"You have one if you want one darling." He squeezed her hand.

An unkind thought whizzed through my head.

If it takes them this long to decide on a drink, how long will other major decisions take, like which socks to put on in the morning?

"The survey's on a little laptop," I said as we all entered the venue.

"Oh John I can't do computers." She stated, now aware of the eight laptops facing her. "You do it."

"No, you'll be fine," John assured her.

"Really, I'm useless with these things." She looked at me.

"You'll be fine," John said putting his arm around her shoulders.

"It's really easy," I said taking the touch pen to show her just how easy it was.

"No, John. I really don't think…"

"Don't be silly darling, you'll be fine." John's voice had a slight edge to it.

"I'm not being silly John, I don't know enough about computers to do this."

"I promise you, it's really easy," I said, adding my reassurance.

"No you do it," she pleaded with John.

"No you do it," John said directly.

"Do you want to do it, sir?" I asked John, who was now looking at his new wife in disbelief.

"Yes John, you do it," she pleaded again.

"No, Cathy you told the lady you'd do it." John sounded sterner.

"John please you do it." Her gaze was desperate.

I wanted to scream "Would one of you do it!" but instead, I said, "If you're not happy about it don't worry."

"I can't believe you're not even going to try," John exclaimed.

"It's not that," Cathy tried to explain.

"It is that, Cathy. You told this lady you'd do the survey, now you saying you won't even try." John was clearly cross.

"It really doesn't matter." I could see this was getting worse.

"It does matter," John answered me back without removing his stare from Cathy. "I can't believe she's not even going to try."

"John, don't take that tone with me."

"It was the same in Jamaica. You wouldn't try the lobster, just because you hadn't had it before."

Oops. Maybe not the perfect honeymoon after all.

"I can't believe you brought that up." Cathy's face flushed red.

"Well for God's sake," John huffed.

There was what I think is called a pregnant pause. I think it was more like an elephant's pregnancy pause, because it seemed to go on forever.

"Don't worry about the survey," I stuttered.

"Maybe that's a good idea as she's not willing to even have a go," John spat towards Cathy rather than replying to me.

Cathy's eyes began to fill with tears.

"It's really beastly of you to bring that up again."

"Well, not to even try." John rolled his eyes. "I mean I couldn't believe you wouldn't even try it, now this."

"Don't worry," I interjected in my smoothest voice. "Don't worry about the survey if you're not comfortable with it."

"I'm sorry we've wasted your time," John almost shouted at me as he turned to leave.

"No that's fine," I stuttered, taken back by his tone.

Cathy said nothing, following him out of the door and down the six flights of stairs we had just climbed. The assent had been as if they were joined at the hip. Now they walked out of the venue as if strangers, Cathy red eyed, John on some sort of mission, striding alone.

My colleague, Neville, who had just entered the room, must have passed them as they left, "Another satisfied customer," he smiled.

"Yeah, but think how much fun they'll have making up." I winked at him, and I thought back to the very first argument I'd had with Peter after we'd been married a couple of weeks. As with all arguments it was over something stupid, an old tape player my dad had given Peter. Peter was thrilled with this new toy. It was a reel to reel, very high tech in its day.

Peter had been messing about with for most of the weekend, taping every LP we owned. I then discovered he had taken our last £15 out of the bank account to buy a micro-phone plus another bit, the name of which I can't remember. It was meant to enhance something or other. When he explained, I was furious. Not only had he not checked with me first, but he had been playing with the dam thing all day, ignoring me. I did some screaming and stated the marriage was now over. Peter remained Mr Cool throughout the whole thing, which caused me to rant on ever more. There's nothing more annoying than someone who won't take the bait and argue back.

I packed some clothes in my duffle bag, slammed the door and walked up the road in the rain, hid in a doorway and waited. Peter came out a few minutes later calling my name. After making him suffer for half an hour longer, I magnanimously forgave him. The making up was as fun, as I'm sure it would be for John and Cathy – at least I hope it would be, because the other alterative is divorce. What would the judge say as they explained the reasoning for the break-down of their short marriage. "Well there was this market research woman and she made me see what he was really like." I hoped that this would be unlikely.

How To Purchase A Car Badly

The diversity of market research is amazing, and yet, it's also something I still can't get use to. One day you're asking members of the public about washing powder, the next it can be on life style. Part of our work can be doing a mystery shop. This entails going along to shops, banks, or even the passport office, and pretending to be a customers or a potential customer. After using their services, you then write a report detailing what the place looked like, whether it was it clean and tidy, how you were dealt with, and so on.

A lot of interviewers don't like doing this sort of work. They feel that you're acting a bit like Big Brother, which is one way of looking at it. But as our own work is always back checked to ensure that we did complete a said interview and that it was completed correctly, I see no reason why other industries don't have some sort of quality assurance check done.

My first ever mystery shop was a bit of a hash up, mainly due to me. I was asked if I would visit a car showroom and pretend to be looking to buy a new car. When the office phoned me with this new type of work, I explained that my knowledge of cars was somewhat like my knowledge of space ships, that being zero. My own car is a V/W but other than the colour, red, I don't know anything about it. Don't know the engine size, what type of fuel it takes. Peter on the other hand is a car fanatic. He can tell you what type pressure is required, how many cylinders it has. More annoyingly, he tends to recognise people by their cars, something I have never understood or comprehended. Whenever we have bought a new vehicle, it's Peter that goes along to sort out the details. I don't even go for the test drive. I'm happy to just go along and collect my new car, which my loving husband will maintain and refuel for me, as necessary. Maybe I'm a bit of a girlie but it's just how we have always done it.

The office reassured me that it wouldn't be a problem, as in car dealer showrooms the car's names are on the number plates. It would be simple. I would walk in, easily recognise the type of car I was pretending to purchase by its name which would, of course, be displayed on the number plate. I agreed to do it.

Driving to the car showroom I was mentally running through the scenario I had been given. I was supposed to be looking to replace my present car for a similar one. I wasn't purchasing today, just having a look at the deals that were around. It would be a cash purchase, so no HP involved. Couldn't be simpler.

Parking behind the showroom, I checked in the mirror to see that my make-up was OK. As I got out of the car my stomach turned, making a small gurgling sound. I was nervous. Taking a deep breath, I walked towards the large glass door at the front of the show room.

As I walked in the smell unique to car showrooms hit my nostrils, sort of like a new carpet had just been laid, combined with not a car-oily smell but a hint of rubber, sort of tyre I suppose. To one side of the showroom, a row of glass panelled offices, in front of them were two light blue sofas with a small coffee table with a scattering of car magazines for those who wanted to flick through to see this year's new colour range for cars – what horse power was available in various models, and of course, the gorgeous leggie ladies with their highly coloured lip gloss, pouting as they leaned over the bonnet of this year's must-have vehicle.

I was in trouble. Why had I agreed to do this? I wouldn't know your V8 engine compared to one that you had to crank with a handle, or why some cars run on diesel or petrol. All I knew was when you filled my car up it was the pump with the black handle.

Play it like a sweet middle-aged women who needs a bit of help, I thought as my tummy made a gurgling sound once again.

"Can I help you?" smiled the charming young salesman as he approached me from one of the glass offices.

"Yes I'm looking for... I'm looking for..." I needed to check my mystery shop notes, as the name of the car I was supposed to be buying had completely slipped my mind.

What was it...? A Z901? Or was it P45? No, idiot, that's a tax form. Why don't they call cars after people? I could have remembered that.

"I'm looking for..."

"Is it a car for yourself," smiled salesman.

"Yes," I nodded, happy that he had known what to say. "Yes. Just a small run around for me."

"What sort of thing did you have in mind?"

We both walked further into the showroom.

Out of the corner of my eye I saw it. "Focus" it said in lovely shiny new letters on the number plate of the blue car placed in the corner of the showroom. It all came flooding back now. When I read my mystery note I was to ask about a Ford Focus.

"Something like that Focus," I said, pointing to what I would have referred to as a "blue car" that being its colour!

"Oh, our Focus," salesman said. "Yes that would be ideal."

We both walked round the exterior of the car, salesman walking anti-clockwise, me clockwise. It had the feeling of a pack of wolfs circling it prey just before a kill.

I felt the urge to kick the tyres as I'd seen my Dad do several times as a child when he went to buy a second hand car, just to show that I was no amateur and knew my onions, but then thought better of it. Maybe that was something you did when buying second hand cars. Maybe something only men were allowed to do.

Salesman was running through his pitch, none of which made the slightest bit of sense to me. "Blur, blur, blur... nought to sixty in... blur, blur... does fifty five around town... sixty on a run... blur, blue, blur..."

I added the odd, "Oh I see," or "Umm I see," just so he thought I was listening and not just saying the same thing over again. A bit of variety never goes amiss.

"Would you like to sit inside?" he beamed as he opened the driver's door.

"Thanks."

That doesn't sound too technical.

More blur, blur, blur as he explained what each shiny disc and dial did. Then he showed me how to move the seat forward to accommodate my short limbs for a comfortable driving position.

"Well it's seems to be the sort of thing I'm looking for," I said getting out of the car as gracefully as I could now my seat was so far forward my bum was having difficulty getting between the steering wheel and edge of the seat.

"Let me get you some further information," said the salesman as he lead me to the glass office.

"Thanks," I agreed as I followed him.

Once seated in the very plush chair in his glass office, sales man proceeded to produce several glossy broachers on the Ford Focus. "Will you be needing finance to purchase?" he enquired.

"No, no. That won't be necessary," I said at speed

"Oh I see. Will you be trading in your own car?" he enquired.

"Yes, I suppose so. To tell the truth I haven't really thought about it," I said honestly.

"So what type of car do you have?" he asked

"A red one," came back my highly intelligent reply.

"Is it the V/W you arrived in?" he smiled back at me, but I felt sure he would have liked to have laughed out loud.

"Yes," I blushed.

"I think I sold that to your husband. Is that Peter?"

"Yes," I blushed further. He must have sussed me.

He knew Peter. He knew that I never have anything to do with buying motor vehicles, and that I described my car as red. He would have also most probably known that I had no idea what type of fuel I used, only that it was from the black handled pump at the garage. It was obvious I was here to do a mystery shop.

My heart sunk. My cover had been blown.

"So you know Peter?" I managed to get out.

"Oh yes we've sold a few cars to him over the years, in fact Peter was in here only the other day looking for a V/W to replace the one you already have, but he said you would be looking for a six month old car. Guess you'd rather have a new one."

"Well you know. You have to see what's on offer," I tried hard to sound convincing. "Do you have a business card?"

Salesman handed me a card with his details printed in gold on it, along with the glossy brochures.

"Well, thank you so very much," I said, shaking his hand. "You've been most helpful, I'll be in touch."

I left with a bit more speed than I entered the showroom. Salesman's face said it all. He was probably thinking Peter and I were going through a messy divorce. I was there to spend money before a settlement could be made to ensure I got more than my entitlement.

Or worse, Peter had passed away and as a grieving widow I was out spending the insurance money.

I swore under my breath never to agree to take part in any further mystery shops. Well, at least not ones that involved buying a bloody car. The statement, "a red one" was swirling around my head.

How stupid did I sound?

I could hear the conversation in the pub that evening as the salesman told his drinking buddies about this woman who came in to buy a car.

"She described her present car as a 'red one', and was spending her dead husband's insurance money before the poor sod has turned cold. Takes all sorts, I suppose," the disgust in his voice clear as he slurped his pint. His friends would shake their head in sad agreement that I was, indeed a disgraceful woman.

Peter found the whole thing highly amusing when I told him about it that evening.

"I would have paid good money to see that. Can't believe you even thought about kicking the tyres," he said before I hit him with a cushion off the sofa to try to stop him from laughing, but failing badly. Even when he did manage to stop laughing to wipe away a tear, two seconds later he was giggling again.

Nowt As Funny As Folk

Before I started working as a market researcher, I understood that we are all different. We all have different values, understandings, each having a lorry load of things we want out of life. One of my dad's favourite sayings was, 'Everyone's a bit queer, except thee and me and I worry about thee.'

How clever was my Dad

As with all jobs you meet some extremely rude, offensive people and now and then you meet that one person that will upset your entire day, making you forget the other hundred or so lovely people you've spoken to.

For some unknown reason I agreed to work a double shift in Peterborough at a McDonald's. I agreed to do the double shift as they couldn't get any other fool to take the work on. I was to get people's reactions to a recent piece of bad press McDonald's had received in the national newspapers.

I left home at 7.30 in the morning, arriving two hours later to begin my first shift by 9.30. Half the work was to be carried out in the actual restaurant bit, the other half to be conducted by the drive through. It was a freezing cold day so I was grateful that the first bit was inside. The second part was not so much fun. As I approached the cars in the queues, I had to walk alongside the car and its inhabitants as they chugged their way along, sometimes waiting while the driver spoke to the intercom box, ordering three Happy Meals – "With the same toy in please so the kids in the back didn't fall out – two burgers, one without cheese, and, yes, the drinks." After they were done, I was able to conduct the interview. The wind was howling and it was a full time job to keep the paper survey in place on my clipboard, as it would rather have been free as a kite and happier to have blown away on a journey around the car park. The respondents in the cars were very kind, I think taking pity on this small woman battling with not only her paperwork, but her coat flapping in the wind and her scarf sometimes covering her view, as they sat waiting to place their order, answering my questions as we moved forward.

At 3.30 my first shift had finished. The staff at McDonald's took pity on me as I returned to the restaurant in a huddled state, my hair blow in various directions with no resemblance of the style I had set out with that morning, my eyes blurred, make-up streaked down my cheeks, shivering from the cold, they kindly offered me a coffee and something to eat. Normal I have to admit that I am not a great lover of McDonald's food, but I gratefully accepted their hospitality, munching on the burger, sipping the piping hot black coffee, as the circulation came back into my feet, relaxing my strained lower back as I warmed up.

After a quick visit to the loo to try and get some sort of order back into my appearance, failing badly to achieve this, I returned to the restaurant to commence my second shift, at 4.00 pm, deciding that a better way to work this inside and outside job would maybe be to do half an hour in, then half an hour outside. Maybe then I wouldn't be chilled to the bone, coming in to have a warm now and then.

The weather was getting progressively worse. The howling wind had brought its friend the rain along with it. Now I was looking even more attractive than I had during the first shift, my hair hanging limply around my face as it was now having its third rinse of the day from the overhead down pour. Going back inside the rainwater dripped from my coat onto the floor.

Why did I agree to take this second shift?

I had decided after 5.00 that I would no longer work outside near the drive through. It was pitch black out there and I just didn't feel safe or happy working on that corner. I knew the staff were only a call away, but I wasn't prepared to take that chance. The company would have to be happy with the numbers I'd completed for the drive through.

By 8 that evening my lower back was on fire and my neck was stiff from hunching my shoulders earlier, in an unsuccessful effort to keep out the cold. Making an executive decision, I decided to take a short break. Again the staff kindly came to my aid, giving me more hot black coffee. After ten minutes it was back to work. Only another two hours to go.

Nine thirty arrived and I only need one more interview before I was done. The restaurant was empty apart from the young girl who had given me that wonderful coffee. She was busy piling the chairs on top of the table and sweeping the floor.

"Been a long day for you," she smiled. "You were here when I arrived at two."

"Umm," I managed.

"Take a seat. I'll get you a coffee," she offered.

"Thanks," I smiled back with true gratitude.

"There you are," she said, placing the paper cup down on a table. "Sit here and take the weight off your feet." She pulled one of the chairs off the table.

I slumped down with the sudden realisation that my back was now broken in several places. It had to be for the amount of discomfort I was in. I tensed my back which did nothing to relieve the burning sensation.

"Thanks ever so much." I smiled up at her.

As I took two sips of the coffee a family came into the restaurant, followed moments later by a second family. I noticed they all had a glowing tan. Sitting there while they placed their order at the counter, I overheard from their conversation that they had just returned from a holiday. I smiled as a couple of them looked over in my direction.

As I finished my coffee, they too had finished their meals. Surely one of them would do a survey, then I would be done.

"Excuse me," I began as I approach their table. "I'm conducting some market research for McDonald's. Would one of you be kind enough to take part in a survey?"

"Go on Sid, you can help the lady out," Sid's mate volunteered him.

"Go on then luv. What do you want to know?"

"Thank you," I said going straight into the first question.

The survey completed, I thanked them, turned to say thanks to the young girl at the counter for keeping me supplied with refreshment, but then I heard it.

"Wish I could get a job like yours," grinned the woman who I suspect was Sid's wife. "Sitting on my bum all day sipping coffee."

I turned. I was tired, every bit of my body ached, and I still had a two hour journey home. My days work wasn't over yet. Something was going to be said.

"Yeah it's great. And I get paid for it." I couldn't keep the sarcasm out of my voice.

The girl behind the counter stifled a giggle.

"Well how rude," Sid's wife snorted.

I couldn't be bothered anymore, thanking the staff yet again I climbed into my car and drove home, blurry eyed. Peter was standing at the door when I pulled in.

"Are you OK Shelley?" he asked taking my bag, clipboard and coat from me.

"Yeah, just tired," I smiled back.

"I've run you a bath," said my oh so wonderful husband.

"Oh Peter," I managed before bursting into tears.

"What's happened?" Peter hugged me closely.

"Nothing," I spluttered. "I've been sitting on my bum all day."

Then the sobs came.

Why had her words got to me? Normally I would have brushed over them. I was also cross at myself for rising to her stupid comments, but driving home that night they had played on my mind. Peter listened patiently as I rambled. How stupid I'd been to take the bait. His sound advice was that I was never to take a double shift again, or better than that give up the bloody job. Yes, I agreed no more double shifts, well until someone asked me. Sid's wife probably didn't even mean it the way I had taken it. It was just a thoughtless remark. Well. I like to think so.

Thank You For Coming Back

One bright autumn day I had taken a job in Cambridge. The leaves had begun their slow journey to the floor, leaving the trees to resemble a witches' broom stick having a bad hair day. It was warm as long as you stood in the bright autumn sunshine and the job was easy enough to do, a five minute interview with members of the public about the shopping facilities in Cambridge City Centre. No quota on age, gender or occupation grading, all I had to do was stop Jo Blogs, even if they didn't live in Cambridge, and ask them what they thought of the city and the shops.

I left my car at the Park and Ride. Once in Cambridge city centre, found a part of the street where the sunshine managed to get between the high buildings in front of some seating benches. They would be handy when I needed to have my lunch, which would be a hot dog from a vending stall close by. I could smell the aroma of the hot dogs wafting through the air.

The morning went well because the survey was quick, uncomplicated.

It got to 1.00, time for lunch. The smell of those hot dogs had been playing on my mind since I'd arrived. Sitting on the bench I enjoyed each mouthful of that high calorie treat, the added mustard and ketchup making the whole experience more than enjoyable. I wiped away the crumbs with the paper napkin which had been rolled around the hot dog and checked in my tiny make up mirror for any bit of ketchup I'd missed. I applied a bit more lippie and flicked through the interviews I'd already completed. Eighteen done. Two more and I'd finished for the day. This was a lovely job.

As I stood up to finish my last two interviews, a gang of three builders strolled over, parking their bums on the bench. They too had bought hot dogs, ready to enjoy their lunch break as I had done.

"Excuse me madam, I'm conducting a survey on Cambridge City Centre, do you have a few moments to give me your opinions?" I asked.

"On what," she enquired.

"We're conducting some Market Research on Cambridge City Centre, just about shopping habits and what you generally think about the City," I smiled back at her.

"Oh I see, yes, yes. I'd be happy to do that, but I'm not giving you any personnel information, is that understood?" she said with an air of superiority that slightly annoyed me.

"I do have to ask you your name, address and telephone number for back checking purposes," I explained.

"OK, yes that would be fine, but I'm not giving any financial details." She looked down on my recruitment form.

"No, we don't ask for anything like that." I reassured her. "And your name is Mrs or Miss?"

"Mrs Edith Barret-Smyth," she offered

How did I know it would be a double-barred name?

"Mrs Barret-Smyth," I spoke alound as I wrote it down. "And your address is?"

"Ash Farm, Histon Rd, Cambs CB3 4QX."

"Thank you. Are you happy to give your telephone number?" I asked as politely as I could.

"Yes." She gave me the number.

"Thank you," I said, writing down her details.

"May I ask you age?" I looked up making direct eye contact with her.

"And that is for…?" she asked not deterring from my direct gaze.

"It's just so we get a even balance of different ages to ensure every age group has coverage, opinions from all sectors of the public, as well as all ages." I lied as this was an open quota, but I did need her age for the recruitment sheet.

"Oh I see." Her stare didn't leave mine. "I'm 57."

"Thank you, I would have lied about my own age." I tried to make light of it, but this one wasn't going to smile. This lady was not for turning. She even had a slight look of Margaret Thatcher.

"May I ask the occupation of the Chief Income Earner in your household?"

"Retired," was her quick response. "We're both retired."

"Thank you. Do you receive a pension from you or your husband's previous job and if so what was his job title?" I thought that would be enough of an explanation.

"What do you mean?" she asked bluntly.

"Well we have to ask all social classes." I had phrased it badly.

"No, no, I don't like that term," she steamed. "No I'm not having that, I don't believe in social grading. It's unethical. No I'm sorry but I' not having that."

"Mrs Barrett-Smyth it's just we have a scale," I began.

"No I'm not having that. I told you I wasn't answering any financial questions. No I'm not having that. Now I'm very cross," she said in a highly raised voice.

"Mrs Barrett-Smyth, I'm not asking for your income."

"You see, that's why I don't do these sorts of things. You want too many personal details," she hissed back at me.

I was fed up now. She wasn't listening to a word I was saying. She already had pre-conceived notions before we began the interview. I wasn't asking about her financial aspect. All I needed was her husband's occupation, for God's sakes. Like I was worried how much they had coming into their household. Maybe they were as poor as Church mice – but I doubted it.

"No, I don't like social grading. We are all equal," she screamed.

By now all the passers-by had stopped to listen. The workers on my bench were I had sat not ten minutes before, stared at both of us.

"Look," I said, fed up with her antics. "That's fine, thank you for your time, but if you're not happy we'll stop here."

"Well I want that." Mrs Barrett-Smyth pointed to my recruitment sheet.

"Fine," I said ripping the top sheet with her details on it, handing it to her. It was no good to me without a full interview.

I watched as she happily screwed the top sheet I handed her in her plump little hands.

"Well thank you for your time, Mrs Barrett- Smyth," was all I could muster.

She stormed off.

I could feel the back of my head burning, knowing the workmen on my bench had watched the whole episode, as had the small crowd who had gathered while Mrs Barrett-Smyth had shouted the odds. I didn't need this, the thirty people or so I'd spoken to earlier, had all been extremely, nice and polite, even if they didn't take part. Mrs Barrett-Smyth was a pain in the arse. She'd made me feel two inches tall and had not listened to a word I'd said. How come she would be the one I would remember and think of? She had made me want to stop working on the easiest of jobs, go home, suck my thumb and say "sod it" to a job I enjoyed.

"Don't know how you do your job," I heard a voice came from behind me.

I turned to see one of the workmen smiling at me.

"She was that sort," he grinned before I could answer. "You handled it very well."

"Thanks," I grinned back.

"You go girl," he smiled as he walked away.

I don't know who he was, but I will be eternally grateful. He inspired me to carry on when I felt demoralised by bloody Mrs Barrett-Smyth. Mr Builder, whoever you are, thank you.

"I'm so sorry," I turned to see Mrs Barrett-Smyth.

"Sorry," I stuttered

"I'm so sorry. I have had the worst day ever. I shouldn't have been so rude," she began. "It's my mother. She's very ill. It's all very complicated..."

"Don't worry," I said suddenly feeling very sorry for this small plump women standing in front of me.

"Please let me explain."

"Really there's no need."

"There's every need. I am truly sorry for the rude way I just spoke to you." Her tone was genuine. "After all, I know you're only doing a job. Please, say you forgive me."

I was now beginning to feel guilty for the awful things I'd been thinking about her. At least she had had the decency to come back and apologize.

"There's really no need. We all have bad days," I smiled back at her.

"There is as I said every need, I am truly sorry."

"I accept you apology then. Thank you for coming back. I do really appreciate it."

I took her hand, which was trembling.

"That is most generous. I expect you get enough abuse from the general public. I shouldn't have added to it." She held my hand tightly.

I almost felt the urge to cuddle her, to reassure her that it was nothing.

"It's fine," was all I could manage as I now felt very emotional also.

"Can I redo the survey?" she almost pleaded.

"There's really no need," I assured her.

"No please, I feel…" Her words trailed off.

"Really it doesn't matter," I said, hoping that this wouldn't offend her. "Anyway I've completed my quota."

"Then please allow me to buy you a coffee or something," she offered.

I thought about turning this kind offer down, but by looking into her face realised that this was her olive branch. It would make her believe she was truly forgiven.

"That would be lovely," I agreed.

We went to a small tea room. At first I sat feeling very awkward, not knowing what to say, but once the tea arrived, we were sitting chatting as if we had been lifelong friends.

Mrs Edith Barrett-Smyth tuned out to be one of the most interesting people I have ever met. She asked me many questions about market research and how I'd gotten into it, showing a keen interest in hearing about my family. I in turn asked her about her family and her interests.

The couple of hours we spent together in that sweet little tea room was so enjoyable to both of us we exchanged telephone numbers with a promise to do it again, which we have many times since, now being firm friends. It was her suggestion that I write a book about the goings on in market research, as she laughed with me as I told her one or two tales.

As I pass through life, I sometimes think of all the people you meet, how you met them, why some turn out to be lifelong friends. I've always been very lucky. All of my friends are just the nicest people, as is Edith Barrett-Smyth.

He's Not My Husband

It was the middle of summer, one of those scorching hot days when the sun is out to melt you. The heat can deterred the public from taking part in a survey, and who can blame them? The choice of where you stand is the essence of getting the job done or not. I always like to seat my respondents down, where ever possible, on a bench if working in the street. Not only am I more relaxed, but after the first couple of questions, they are too. When I arrive at the location at which I'm to work, my first job is to check out the seating arrangements of the town centre, placing myself close by to a bench. My wording is probably a bit naff but it makes most people smile.

"Thanks," I say after they've agreed to take part. "This is my office. Would you like to take a seat?" I point to the given bench.

It sort of breaks the ice.

The survey I was working was about life styles – quite an interesting one, but it was hot. People wanted to do their bit of shopping then get home. The day would be challenging.

I approached several people. All of them declined politely. Then I saw her walk up the street toward me and I somehow knew she'd do it.

"Excuse me madam, I'm conducting some market research. Would you be willing to take part?"

"Yes of course, but can we sit down, the heat is really getting to me." She gestured to my bench. I wouldn't have to use my corny line.

She carefully placed her many shopping bags against her on the bench as I explained the run of the mill stuff, roughly what the survey was about, and also that all her personal details wouldn't be passed on to any third party, taking her name address and telephone number.

"How many times do you use public transport?" I asked the first question.

"Not that often really. Sometimes I catch the bus if the car is off the road."

"So about once every so often," I said pointing to the show cards which gave respondents various choices.

"Yes, about that. Well maybe not even that often." She pointed to "less often" on my show card.

"How many trips do you make to the city centre in a month?" I asked, without looking up.

"About once a month, I guess." She said this without hesitation.

Once she had answered several questions, she turned into the type of respondent that is every market researcher's dream. Her answers were direct. There was no "well I don't know" and given the choice of "strongly agree", "slightly agree", "slightly disagreed", or "strongly disagree", she didn't just say yes but said if she strongly agreed of didn't. I had no need to prompt her for any answers. Nearing the end of the survey, I became aware that a man around about her age was standing in front of us. Looking up, I smiled at him. He was clutching a Tesco's bag tightly in his hand, raised level with his shoulder.

"I've just been to Tesco's," he announced, grinning from ear to ear.

I smiled back at him, as did my respondent.

"I bought these," he said proceeding to take each item from the carrier bag.

We both watched as he showed us a tin of Value own bake beans, a packet of digestive biscuits, and tube of toothpaste.

We both looked on, smiling as he produced each item. I thought she must have given him a list of things to get while she had popped somewhere else, before being stopped by me. He was checking with her that he had achieved his shopping mission correctly, the way most husbands do. Without warning, after placing his recent purchases back into the carrier bag, he then burst in song.

"You are the sunshine of my life," he began at the top of his lungs.

I thought it was sweet of him to serenade his wife in this way, but his singing voice was hardly the calibre of Mr Steve Wonder.

"That's why I'll always be around," he warbled.

I was now feeling quite embarrassed for not only her, but him.

A crowd was gathering to watch this elderly man singing, Tesco's carrier bag still held at shoulder height, giving it his all, perspiring somewhat in the glare of the sunshine.

I moved my glaze from him to look down at my clipboard.

"No, no, look at me," he spluttered, pausing half way through his off-key singing.

I did as I was instructed, returning to stare back at him as he continued, now undeterred by my rudeness by having the cheek to look away.

"You are the sunshine of my lifffffe!" He finished.

Without another word he turned and walked away, Tesco's carrier bag still held high.

I was lost for word, but felt the need to say something, "That was sweet of your husband." I managed.

"He not my husband," my respondent looked startled that I should think such a thing. "I don't know who he is."

I was relieved for her that she was not married to a lunatic, but also slightly embarrassed that I had thought she was. I was also worried that he was allowed to wander the streets.

When I told Peter the story he couldn't believe that it was true.

"You certainly know how to pick them, Shelley," he giggled.

Body Functions

My family love to hear the tales I have told them after returning from work. Our son Lawrence finds it all a bit hard to believe, if I am telling him of the latest funny.

"You should really write a book about all of this, Mum," he said one afternoon when he'd popped round to see me. "Mind, no one would believe the stories."

"They're all true," I promised.

"Yeah, but no one would think so many crazies were around," Lawrence said cutting his second slice of cake, giving me a sideways glance with his impish grin to check I didn't mind him taking it.

"Maybe I should write one on you." I used my stern Mother's voice.

"Naw, no one would believe you had such a wonderful son," he grinned.

There are certain qualities required, that you need to work as a market researcher. These are:

a pleasant personality, a fairly nice smile, self belief, good timekeeping, and a great SatNav (it doesn't have to be called Drew-Cilla). You have to like people, but most importantly, you need a strong bladder!

Location we are sent to work in, determines how near or far you are from that handy supermarket for a warming cup of coffee, or an essential loo, so a bladder that can wait comes high on the list of priorities necessary to do the job.

Often while interviewing someone in their own home, they will kindly offer you some sort of refreshment. This is something I always decline. You could enjoy a lovely cup of tea or coffee with them in their home, but then three doors further down the street you would suddenly feel the call of nature, with the possibility of nowhere to go. You can ask the next respondent's you interview if you could use their loo, but although I know some interviewers will do this, it's not something I feel comfortable with.

Then of course some houses we go into you just wouldn't want to use their facilities. It's at these not so well kept homes that they usually say as you step over the threshold, "Do excuse the mess. I haven't clean up today."

I always think, *TODAY. Don't you mean all year?* as I step over old cartoons of food or clothing thrown anywhere.

Should you need to answer the call of nature, it usually involves go back to your car and driving a few miles to find the nearest loo, be it in a supermarket or department store, or garage. If this isn't possible you have to find a wooded area, again something I personally am not happy about, finding it difficult to feel relaxed being sort of exposed, a sentiment my fellow interviewer Tara felt similarly about when telling me of her experience.

Tara, a seasoned interviewer, was working on a public interest survey. Should have been a really easy job to do, however the day she was booked to undertake her work was one of those days in British history. The wind howled, the rain stormed down and it even hailed at one point. It was the worst day possible to try and complete a door to door survey. On days like this, if you arrive at someone's doorstep soaking wet, who is going to invite you in? Sadly for Tara, no one wanted to answer her questions. She plodded round for a couple of hours. Then, dripping from head to toe, she decided to return to her car, soaked to the skin, pissed off and now in need of a loo.

Now, a market researcher's car often resembles a skip, not one of the tidiest places in the world. After all, we spend hours in our cars travelling, filling in our paperwork as we go, more often than not eating our lunches in there. Our cars are not only our form of transport, they are our offices, our restaurants, and our shelter should the heavens open. And yet, we never seem to want to clean them. You will find several types of clothing either slung on the back seat or piled in the boot. In my own car, I have three pairs of different types of shoes, four coats, and a couple of hats. You have to have this variety of clothing in case the place you arrive at to work has different weather to where you've just come from. Of course there are always loads of pens rolling round the floor, plus receipts from petrol stations, which you promise yourself you'll take out at the end of the day, along with any packaging from your lunch. Upon arriving home, carrying so much other paperwork from the job you've just done, a simple receipt isn't on your propriety list, nor that plastic container that had your sandwich in. So they tend to clutter the car seats or floors for many weeks, maybe even months, until our army of thoughtful husbands or partners catch a glance of the insides of our cars, tut, and promptly empty them for us.

Tara now trudged back to her car, throwing her soaking wet clip board, bag and soggy paperwork on the back seat. Miles from anywhere she sat in the driver seat staring out, as the wind howled and the rain flew in torrents against the windscreen.

There was nothing for it. She had had a wasted a 40 mile trip. No one wanted to have a dripping market researcher standing on their nice clean floor making puddles big enough for a family of ducks to plunge into. Tara was just going to have to cut her losses and go home, but first she had to, *had* to, find a loo – and soon.

Turning her car round she began mentally retracing her journey to the tiny village she had been told to visit to complete the surveys. Had there been a Tesco's or a Sainsbury's anywhere, she could possibly have had a pee. As she drove down the rain drenched windy lanes the urge of nature began to increase. Tara wiggled in her seat, her right leg bouncing up and down. "Think of something else," she told herself as she listened to the swish of the water as her car drove through the road side puddles. Half an hour later she was still in the depths of the countryside, not a hint of civilisation. Not even a Tesco's Express, which, let's face it, are everywhere. Mr Tesco's was slipping – a missed opportunity. "There must be a garage," she thought as she turned the next corner, but no nothing.

Tara looked round her car in desperation. On the floor on the passenger's side she spied her saving grace, a plastic container, left from one day last week, when Tara had enjoyed a triple English breakfast sandwich, along with a freshly squeezed bottle of orange juice when taking a well deserved lunch break in her car.

A lane appeared to the left, Tara swerved into it. It was isolated. No one about. But then, who other than a market researcher would venture out on a horrible day? Parking the car Tara frantically grabbed the triple breakfast container. It would be perfect. Throwing her wet coat over her lap she proceeded to pull down her trousers and knickers, placing the triple breakfast container appropriately. Then, with the greatest of relief, she let flow. It was wonderful, a strange peacefulness passing over Tara's face. Seconds later, the peace turned to concern. She had been waiting so long, she was unsure if the flow would ever stop, and while to container was fairly large, Tara wondered if it was going to be man enough for the job. Then, a miracle happened. Tara's wee stopped not a moment too soon, just before it overflowed from the top of the container.

"Thank God," she whispered under her breath.

Two seconds longer, and the consequences didn't bare thinking about.

Now all that remained was the delicate task of removing the container from under her without spilling a drop.

"Idiot," Tara rebuked herself. "Why didn't you sit on the passenger side?" She negotiated the difficult task of lifting her bum to enable her to easy the triple sandwich container from underneath her.

Not a drop was spilt. Pleased with her efforts, Tara opened the driver's door, ready to flick the contents out over the field. Whoosh went to gust of wind as it caught the door. "Fuck," said Tara as the container somersaulted, emptying its entire contents into the driver's side door pocket.

Tara watched in amazement as a few sparse bubbles appeared, followed by a floating pen, then a rather soggy petrol receipt bobbed its way to the top of the yellow liquid.

It took some time for Tara to collect her thoughts, clean up the mess as best she could, then drive the 40 odd miles home.

"It's been an eventful day," she said to herself as she poured a glass of wine, once home.

White Van Man

Friends often ask, "Do you ever get worried about some of the people you interview?"

I suppose they have a point, I do truly believe that most people are nice and caring and that they have no more wish to do harm to you than you do to them.

Working with the public is a two way street. If you're working on a door to door job, they have to trust you are who you say you are, allowing you into their homes – although there are those who will only do a survey standing at the door step. Fair enough if that's what they prefer. They are kind enough to do the survey – although it's sometimes nicer if you are invited in on a cold day. I would say that most of the time you can judge people from first impressions, not always but most of the time, so if you talk to them for a few moments at the doorway you can get a feel of what they are like, generally speaking,

If at anytime I felt uncomfortable or threatened, I would leave, as you always make sure of a getaway route.

I had a supervisor I worked for quite a lot. I enjoyed the type of work she gave out as it was always varied, interesting and fun to do. Plus she was more than fair getting you the best fee she could.

"Hi, Elaine. How are you?" I asked recognising her voice.

"Great. Got a great job for you," Elaine announced down the phone.

"OK sounds, good." I liked Elaine's work. It was always interesting.

"It's working in Cambridge," she began. "Getting men who drive vans to take part in an email survey later in the week. They get £40 for taking part."

"When's it got to be done by?"

Elaine went on to explain dates, pay structures, etc. All I had to do was drive down to Cambridge, find some fellows in vans, ask them if they would do an email survey later in the week, and they got £40. What could be easier?

On the allotted day, I jumped into my little red car and trundled down the A11 towards Cambridge. It was a reasonably bright day but it looked like it would turn to rain later. Not that it would bother me. I would either be sitting in my cars or sitting in some fellow's van.

Pulling off the slip road, I saw my first port of call. A white transit van parked in a lay-by plus a bonus van parked in front of it. Better safe than sorry – not that anyone would attack me, little middle aged woman that I am. But at least there would be someone close by if I did need help.

Knocking on the driver side window, the driver looked up from the Sun newspaper he was reading, somewhat startled by a middle aged women complete with clipboard knocking on his window.

As he wound the window down, I went straight into my spiel. "Excuse me, my darling," I beamed, "I'm conducting some market research with van drivers. Just getting your opinions on road usage. It's to take part in an email survey later this week, and as thank you for your time you get £40. Is it something you'd consider, and do you have email facilities?"

"Yeah, I have." van man agreed.

"Brilliant," I smile back, "Can I climb in next to you? It won't take long. I'll just get your details and explain what you have to do."

"OK," van man nodded.

With a bit of effort, I managed to climb the high step into the passenger side of the cab. Sitting next to van man, I ran through what he had to do, getting his details name, address, email.

"Thanks my darling," I said looking down from the lofty height of the cab, to the tarmac of the lay-by. Taking a deep breath, I took the death defying leap from cab to road, catching my elbow as I tumbled, gracefully, of course.

"Bye." I heard van man say.

Cor, this is going to be a lovely, nice, easy peezy job.

The interview had taken all but a few moments and van man was happy to be getting £40.

"Lovely work. Thanks Elaine." I whispered to myself.

As the day progressed, apart from startling a few van drivers wondering what on earth this middle aged women was doing knocking on their van windows, it was going like a dream. Well apart from me bruising my elbows each time I hurled myself out of the vans. All the van drivers were friendly, and happy to take part to get their money. Lovely way to spend a day.

Around one o'clock, I decided I earned myself a lunch break. Peter, bless him, had prepared some sandwiches for me. While he had been buttering the bread that morning, he'd given me the pep talk about the dangers of jumping in and out of strange men's vans. I had promised to take every precaution, to ensure my safety. I promised, my hand on my heart, I would only jump into a van if it was in a built up area or if there was someone else close by.

"Anyway, who do you think would carry me off?" I said getting bored with his concerns.

"Shelley, don't be stupid." Peter looked cross "You're a very attractive woman..."

I looked over at my adorable husband, thinking how lucky I was I'd bagged him.

Leaning over, I planted a kiss on his lips. "Peter, I will be careful."

"Just make sure you are," he said.

Munching through the delicious sandwich, I thought I had better text Peter, to let him know that I was OK. Tell him my safety wasn't an issue, and that, if anything, it was the getting in and out of the vans which was causing me problems. Cursing my short legs as I fell to the floor each time I descended from a van.

Brushing the bread crumbs from my top, I looked up. Bugger. It had started to rain. Just a few droplets, but the sky had turned very dark, there would be a downpour to follow. As I gazed through the windscreen I saw a young bloke, about thirtyish, walking from a warehouse toward his white van. He was well built, and I guessed worked out at a gym given his frame and bulging muscles. Without thinking, I threw the rest of my lunch onto the back seat of the car, jumped out and ran over to him.

"Excuse me my darling," I began. "I'm doing some market research with van drivers. Is that your van over there?" I pointed towards what I had anticipated was his vehicle.

"Yeah." he looked very surprised being accosted by a little old lady.

"I'm looking for fellows who drive vans to take part in a survey about roads. The survey is done via email. Is that something you'd be interested in doing? They pay you £40 as a thank you for your time."

Mr. Muscle gave me a sideways glance, "You're going to give me forty quid for doing a survey?"

"Not me, my love. The company I work for are giving it to you as a thank you."

He nodded. "OK then. I'm up for that."

We were standing half way between his van and my little red car and at that moment, the heavens had decided to open up.

"Do you want to sit in my car or your van, just while I get your details?" I asked.

"Don't mind." Mr Muscle replied.

"My car it is then," I said leading the way.

Once we'd sat down in my car, I asked him the small amount of information required.

"Your name is?"

"Martin, Martin Stephenson."

"Thank you." I said writing his name on the questionnaire. "And your email address?"

Nothing.

"Martin you do have email, don't you?" I looked up.

Mr Martin Stephenson, otherwise known as Mr Muscle sat in silence, his hands cupped in his lap.

"Martin, are you OK?"

Martin turned, looked me straight in the eye, his cheeks flushed with embarrassment. "Look misses," he said. "You aren't going to drive off with me are you?"

It took me a moment to collect my thoughts. I suppressed the giggle rising within me.

"No Martin, I'm not going to drive off with you. To tell the truth, darling, I can't breathe in for that long anymore."

We both let out a healthy giggle. Mine as I wondered what Martin thought I was going to do to him. Martins I think, from relief.

He later rang me and thanked me for getting him the £40.00, which was thoughtful.

KGB Agent

It's always nice to work with someone else as the job can be a lonely one if it's just you. I was once again working on the Transport Department contract, gathering data on peoples cycling movement in Cambridge, one of my work mates who had now become a close and valued friend along with her husband, was working alongside me. Linda and I had decided it would be nice to share the work. We had pre-selected address to go to, so we decided she would take one side of the road to be worked on and I would take the other. The survey was pretty straight forward. No awkward questions, just how often do you cycle – if you do, how many people in the house cycle, that sort of thing. The only difficult question and I would use that term loosely was, was which ethnical back ground do you come from, but given the very many different backgrounds in Cambridge, it wasn't a real problem.

Linda is the sweetest of lady's, she won't mind me saying but she looks as if she should be enrolled in the Women's Institute. She has a wicked sense of humour, finding the slightest funny thing in various situations we find ourselves in. She can use the internet, selling items on eBay for profit, but for some undetermined reason cannot master a cell phone.

Working on this job it was important that we could contact each other to say whereabouts we were or how many interviews we had completed, so that both of us understood the place we were at with regards to the job. I would phone Linda while out on the street, to inform her of which address I had completed, just so she would not do a double call there, only to find her cell phone switched off, swearing under my breath, but still loving her.

On one trip to Cambridge, Linda was sitting next to me in the car as we parked in one of the streets we were to work door to door. My phone went off. Picking it up, I glanced at the caller's name. "Linda's mobile" it read. I looked across at her, perplexed.

"What?" she asked.

"Don't you want to talk to me face to face?" I enquired keeping a straight face.

"What?" Linda looked puzzled.

"Linda you're calling me on my phone," I pointed to my phone in my hand. "And I'm sitting right next to you."

"Oh must have left it on," she leant over to pick up her handbag to terminate the call.

I couldn't stop laughing for ten minutes, nor could Linda. Bless her cotton socks, she still to this day doesn't know how to put the lock on her phone, pick up messages, also getting confused as to why all her credit has gone when she's only just bought it a few days before. I have explained it's because she kicks or presses it while it's in her bag. Most probably she's phoned Western Australia every now and then. No wonder she's never got credit!

Working this job in Cambridge I knew one thing: I could rely on Linda. She was hard working and did a good job. It was just the cell phone I couldn't get her to use.

On a nice bright day in late September I parked near to the river. We both gathered our paperwork and got out of the car after deciding who would take which side of the road. We agreed to phone each other when we had finished a couple of interviews, in case it was necessary to swap sides of the road, should we run out of addresses on the side we were working.

"Just one thing, Linda," I said sternly. "Put your bloody phone on." I smiled.

Linda smiled back, while fumbling in her handbag to check it was on. She put her thumb up to assure me it was "wilco over and out". I did the same.

Walking up and down the street and checking my list to find the right address allocated to me, I knocked on my first door. This job was lovely because everyone so far had been happy to do a survey, given they had time. Cycling was apparently a subject close to their hearts.

The door opened and I went into my explanation of why I was on their door step. Yes this lady would do it.

Second address the response was the same.

I was just going to the third house when my phone went. It was Linda. "Shelley can you come now? I'm at number 19. Then I heard a bit of shouting in the background break out.

"OK be there in a moment," I shouted in case Linda couldn't hear me above the noise.

I swivelled to face the right direction to get back to Linda. Within moments I could see her standing by a front door, the owner I assumed standing in the doorway: a very large lady, with white hair, waving her arms around. Linda was standing on the doorstep arguing with her.

"Hello," I said in my calmest voice.

"Hello," said the lady in the doorway, putting out her hand for me to shake, which I did.

"There's a problem, Shelley." Linda sounded terrible shaken. "This lady doesn't believe we're market researchers."

"Oh." I tried to sound matter-of-fact. "And you are?"

"Miss Underwood," she volunteered.

"Miss Underwood, I can assure you that we are both working as market researchers." I was charm itself. "I'm sure Linda has told you we are working for the Transport Department."

"I believe you, but I don't think *she* is," Miss Underwood snarled in Linda's direction.

"Now, Miss Underwood, I can assure you that we are both..."

"This is my superior." Linda threw in. Why, I was unsure.

"We are both working throughout Cambridge gathering data for the Transport Department," I started again, still wondering why Linda seemed to think I was her superior.

"So you're both in on it," Miss Underwood exclaimed, turning her anger towards me.

"Miss Underwood, we both have appointments, could we call back later to discuss this?" I suggested.

"Do you promise to call back?" she demanded.

"I can assure you we will do everything in our power to do so," I said not wishing to make a promise I knew we would not be keeping.

"Where are you parked?" Miss Underwood enquired.

My mind raced, my car was opposite the house, parked close to the river Cam. She seemed nuts. If I told her where I'd parked

I might come back to a car pushed into the river, tail lights just showing above the waves.

"A couple of streets away," I lied.

As I said these words a chap of about the same age as Miss Underwood appeared beside me.

"Excuse me ladies, I am Miss Underwood's brother," he announced. "My sister is not very well."

I wanted to say, "Do you think," but that wouldn't have been kind.

"Oh I see," I said. "We'll, leave you to it then." I shook his hand and we left.

Turning the corner Linda began to laugh, the laughter of relief I think.

"I need a coffee," she admitted.

Sitting in the little pub we had found earlier that week Linda explained what had happened.

Linda had knocked on the door of the address we had been allocated. Miss Underwood had opened the door and invited her in, Linda struggling to show her I.D. as she entered the premises, Miss Underwood not the slightest bit interested in seeing it.

As Linda walked through the door she happened to mentioned in passing "Oh it's chilly today isn't it." making small talk.

"I'll get you a blanket," Miss Underwood announced as she swept past Linda, disappearing for only a moment, returning with a bright pink fluffy blanket, which she proceeded to wrapped around Linda, in a cocooned fashion, leaving Linda's arms free to cling onto her clip board and paperwork.

"Do take a seat," Miss Underwood pointed to the arm chair behind Linda's mummified body.

"Thank you," Linda said like the true professional, not fazed by being rolled like a mopped herring.

"Now before we start," Miss Underwood stared transfixed into Linda's eyes, "Where do you like to visit?"

"Sorry," Linda replied.

Miss Underwood turned to the large dark wooded table to the right of the chair where Linda had flopped into. "Where do you like to visit?" She pointed to an open map of the world laying upon the table.

"Uh, Cyprus," Linda spluttered.

"Good choice. Now if you write your name on Cyprus, then we can proceed," Miss Underwood beamed.

"Write my name on Cyprus." Linda said as she searched the map for Cyprus and did as she was told. "LIN-DA DRU-MOND," she sounded her name as she wrote.

"Lovely." Miss Underwood clapped her hand in joy. "Now what is it you wish to ask me?"

"Well, this is a survey being conducted by the Transport Department. Here is a letter explaining about it and here is a thank you note about the company I work for. The Transport Department have commissioned us to undertake the survey from people in Cambridge, and this," Linda added as she had been trained to do, "is my I.D."

Miss Underwood took the I.D. card staring at it for several moments, then reading every word on both the Transport Departments letter and the thank you note from the company we were working for. "OK, seems to be in order," she agreed, not noticing that Linda had used this precious time to try and free herself from the bright pink blanket, managing to loosen it somewhat.

"Can I just ask," Linda began, "Have you ridden a bicycle in the last year?"

"I'm not answering that," Miss Underwood spat back folding her ample arms over her equally ample chest.

"Sorry. But why not?" enquired Linda.

"No. No, you're not tricking me into that one," Miss Underwood smirked. "I'm not that stupid."

"Would you rather not take part in the survey," Linda said while managing to untangle herself a little more from that bloody blanket.

"No I didn't say that, just I'm not answering that question."

"OK," Linda sighed. "How many people in the household ride a bicycle?"

"That's my business, isn't it," Miss Underwood answered smugly.

"OK," Linda smiled, while turning to the back page of the survey, missing out most of it.

"Can I ask your ethnic background," Linda said showing Miss Underwood a card with listings of various backgrounds.

Miss Underwood scrutinized the list, her eye lids half closed as she did so.

"No I'm not on there," she announced.

"OK, can I ask you ethnic background?" Linda tried again, then she added, which we are never supposed to do, but in this case was totally allowable, "Are you White British?"

"I don't like that term," Miss Underwood stated. "If you have to put anything put 'A person born of the British Empire'." She beamed with pride. "In fact I demand you write that down."

Linda wisely did as she was told. 'The respondent demanded I wrote this down, she is a person born of the British Empire,' Linda wrote beside the question of ethnic background.

Miss Underwood watched carefully to ensure her instruction were adhered to. "I see you need my name and address." She had read the next section while looking over Linda's shoulder.

"Only if you wish to give them," Linda smiled.

"Well I'll give them to you, but it won't be my true name of course," Miss Underwood smirked again. "It will be one of my names I've used in the past."

"That's fine," Linda agreed.

"Rudolf Hasseltine," Miss Underwood announced.

"Rudolf Hasseltine," Linda wrote down as she said it aloud.

"But that's all I'm giving you. You're not getting my address or telephone number." Miss Underwood grimaced, obviously forgetting that Linda was sitting in her house.

"That's fine, thank you," Linda smiled. "Now I must be on my way, thank you so much, could you help me with this lovely warm blanket," Linda said rising to her feet.

"Were did you say you were from?" Miss Underwood enquired. "What company was it?"

"Prada Research. It's there on the thank you note I gave you, along with that letter from the Transport Department."

"That's what you say, but I think differently. In fact, I know who you are. You think I'm stupid."

"I am who I say I am. If you wish ring the company, our number is right there on the thank you note, or if you would prefer, ring the Department of Transport, there's a number on that letter." Linda's tone was now defiant.

"No, I know who I'll ring, the police. They'll pin a medal on me once they hear I've captured a KGB Agent." Miss Underwood flicked her head backwards as she left the room to go into the hall to phone the police.

Linda said at this point she wasn't sure if she was worried or wanted to laugh out loud, but used these moments to totally free herself of the blanket which had engulfed her for what had seemed an eternity.

By the time Linda reached the hallway, Miss Underwood was standing with the receiver in her hand, holding it towards Linda. "There you are tell them who you are, confess?"

Taking the phone Linda spoke softly into the mouth piece, "Hello my name is Linda Drummond, I'm working in Cambridge for the Transport Department doing a survey on cycling. Miss Rudolf Hassletine thinks I could be a KGB agent, but I'm not," Linda dutifully handed back the phone to Miss Underwood, biting her lip as she did so.

Miss Underwood took the receiver from Linda. "Of course she's lying – unless she works for the United State of America's C.S.I. She could even be from Romania." Miss Underwood stopped there as the police officer on the other end of the line began to give her some sound advice, no doubt while holding back the laughter with difficulty. "OK officer, I understand. I will do my best not to compromise my position. I fully understand what you're saying, thank you." Miss Underwood nodded in agreement with this sensible advice, putting her hand over the mouthpiece. "They say you must stand outside, so as not to compromise my position," she said waving her hand in a backward movement towards Linda.

Linda didn't hesitate to leave, and as she did she rang me.

While Linda told her tale, I had managed to keep a straight face, thinking what could have happened to her, but it was when she showed me the questionnaire with the comments about Miss Underwood demanding she wrote down the things she said I couldn't, just couldn't, hold back the laughter. I think we both stopped laughing about an hour later, people in the pub looking across to see what was so funny, as tears ran down both our faces.

We were not laughing at the clear sadness that Miss Underwood was a very unwell lady. That was a great shame. It was just our way of coping with the situations we find ourselves in. How well Linda had done not panicking. I was proud of her.

We calmed down, then I had to ask, "Why on earth did you call me your superior?" As I did so, I clicked my heel together under the table, this started us off again.

"Tell me one thing," I asked.

"What?"

"How come you managed to use your mobile to call me, when you don't know how to get my number up on your phone?" I questioned.

"Well, maybe I do know how to use them." Linda grinned.

With that we were off again, people staring across the pub wondering why these two middle-aged women were giggling so much and so loudly, they must have thought the diet coke we were both drinking had several large tots of something in it.

Civil Servants And The Like

Checking my diary for the week ahead, one Sunday evening, I noted I was booked to do a train job. Not the sort Ronald Biggs had done. I was to be interviewing passengers while they travelled. This sort of work was OK once you'd established your 'sea legs.' The motion of the train is difficult to get use to. If you were lucky and didn't fall on your respondent while you were interviewing them, that was a bonus.

The day arrived. I travelled to Peterborough to catch the early to York. The interview was to be done on a P.D.A. This marvellous little machine we use to record interviews then sending them back straight away. I was to interview first class passengers only. At least there would be a bit more room to walk up and down in.

Before boarding, to make absolutely sure, I check with not only one but two train guards that I was getting on the right train. Better be safe than sorry Shelley, you don't want to go in the wrong direction.

Once on board I made myself know to the train guard, once again checking that this was the correct train!!!

"If you need anything just give us a shout." He kindly offered.

I was off and running. The first carriage wasn't very busy, just a couple of businessmen working on their laptops.

I gingerly approached the first one, "Excuse me Sir, I'm doing some market research with commuters, would you be willing to spare a few minutes to complete a survey?"

Peering over the top of his glasses, "Yes, don't see why not, take a seat." He gestured with his hand to the seat opposite his.

The survey took all of five minutes. Thanking him I moved to the only other occupant of the carriage. Luckily he also agreed to take part, The Gods were with me today.

Moving on to the next carriage, I tumbled from one side of the walkway to the other, knowing that there would be bruises to follow as I hit tables and chairs. The second carriage was a bit more fruitful, three couples were dotted about, plus seven individual businessman, sat around the carriage. At the far end I could see the top of a chaps head he had his mobile phone pressed to his ear. Because he was talking so loudly everyone in the carriage could hear each and every word he uttered. For his sake, I hoped it was not a personal conversation.

After working my way down the carriage, I was almost done. The chap at the end had finally stopped using his mobile I think much to the relief of the other passengers as well as myself. I was now standing at the table and chair just before his. An old chap sat reading The Times.

I explained what I was doing he kindly agreed to do the survey, inviting me to sit opposite him, which I did.

As I sat there I became aware of the awful eating noises coming from the man sitting behind me, mobile phone man. The extremely loud, crunching followed by slobbering noises, then a horrid gulping sound. Then the uncontrolled burp which echoed throughout the entire carriage. The respondent I was sitting opposite to me twitched his nostrils in disgust. I carried on with the survey, thanking him for his time once it was completed.

As I stood up, turning my eyes met the Monster Muncher, who had not stopped eating, the whole time I had been conducting the last survey. A jolly fine lad he was too, of Friar Tuck proportions. His plump chops bouncing up and down as he devoured more of those complimentary crisps, nuts and biscuits, all washed down with gulps of coffee.

His clothing was expensive, but casual. He eyed me up and down, as I stood beside his chair.

"Yes young lady, what can I do for you?" he said showing a collection of food still in his mouth.

I explained what I was doing.

"OK, that sound allowable, fire away." He said.

Before I could utter the first question, the service trolley rolled towards us.

Monster Muncher's table was littered with empty packs of complimentary goodies. Enough packs lay there to keep a small army going. The trolley assistant rightly assumed he had, had his fill, so therefore passed him by.

"Where do you think your going?" he bellowed at her.

Blushing, she pulled the trolley back to his table. "I'm sorry Sir, what would you like?"

"I'd like," he smirked, "better service, you trolley dolly's need to keep your eye on the ball."

As he was saying this, he stretched over taking handfuls of different treats from the loaded trolley.

"More, coffee." He motioned to his cup.

Dutifully she began to pour coffee into the cup placed on the table.

"Not in there you stupid girl, get a clean one for Christ sake." He hurled at her.

She was now shaking as she handed him a new cup of coffee.

Your, a pig, I thought.

"Now, where were we?" he turned his attention back toward me. His fat greedy hands pulling open a packet of nuts, throwing them into his cake hole it resembled a builder loading a cement mixer.

"Can I ask who paid for your ticket?" I asked the next question.

"Tax payer." He spat food as he replied.

"Tax payers?" I questioned.

"Yeah, I work for the government." He lifted the next lorry load of food to his mouth.

"And how much did you pay for your ticket?" the sight of that food rolling round was making me feel sick.

"Well it was £130 ish but I missed the sodden first train, buying these shoes." He pointed toward his foot, "So had to buy another ticket, I suppose in the end I paid.." he paused to pick something out of his teeth with the nail of his little finger, "I suppose £260, say £290."

I looked at him, even if I was to show my disgust he wouldn't have cared. I was relieved once the survey was completed.

Thinking about our Norwich Labour M.P., who had recently resigned due to the recent expenses scandal, I remembered how sad I was that he had to take such action. Although I do not vote for Labour, I had interviewed him some months before. He seemed like a decent chap. I knew he had done many good works for his constituency. While, the expenses scandal was and is inappropriate, it still seemed a shame he had been made to resign, as he seemed to care. Unlike Mr Monster Munch, who clearly didn't give a damm.

Who's Who.

While I know some surveys can be as interesting as watching paint dry, there are some that are down right boring. We were working on one such as this on a summer's day in Ipswich. It was once again a self completion. We had lost several respondents due to them giving up as it was too long and mind numbingly boring. If a respondent walked out we had to replace them again. While I can't blame anyone from walking away from this particular survey, the day was proving difficult for us as a team.

I finally recruited someone, It felt a bit like taking a lamb to the slaughter, as we walked toward the Town Hall, were the survey were taking place.

Sitting my respondent down, running through the motions, I heard Jo's excited chatter as she walked in. Looking up I saw why. She had recruited a member of a pop group, famous still but they had formed in the 1960's. He was still a dish. He had long shoulder length blond hair, an open necked shirt. Yeah he still had it.

"It's a touch screen, there you go." Jo explained as she wriggled like a school girl.

Our celebrity had no problem picking it up.

"Is that who I think it is?" I asked Jo once outside.

"Yes." She said almost wetting herself.

"Better get someone else so you can make him an other coffee." I giggled.

Luck would have it I managed to recruit someone else. As we walked through the door of the venue Mr Celeb was leaving.

"Do you work for this company?" he enquired.

"Yes I do." I said with pride.

"Well you can tell them from me thats the most boring thing I've ever done."

"Ohhh sorry." Was my meek answer.

He was of course right, at least he'd finished the survey, but hey not everything is, rocking all over the world.

Telephone survey can be difficult. It's easier for someone to refuse on the phone, or even put the phone down on you. Also you have to speak very clearly so they can understand each and every question. I'm not a big lover of phone surveys but will do the odd one or two.

Haley rang me one evening. "Got something different for you." Haley was lovely, very glam. The work she handed out was always fun.

"Ok Hun, what is it." I asked.

"Got some telephone survey's, for a prestigious store in London." Haley announced, "It's getting in touch with their customers to see why they've not used the store credit card in the last six months."

"Am guessing you get a list of their customers?" I questioned.

"Yes of course." Haley agreed.

She went on to discuss pay rate, explaining that the expenses would be £2 per call, more than enough to cover the cost of a five minute telephone interview.

I agreed to take it.

Two days later the work arrived. The customer list a 'Who's Who's' of the rich and famous, with the odd Mr and Mrs thrown in for good measure. This was going to be fun.

Armed with my bestest B B C voice, I rang the first number.

A few moment, someone picked up. "Good morning would it be possible to speak to Lord or Lady Dingdell?"

"Speaking." came the reply.

"Oh, good morning Lady Dingdell my names Shelley, Shelley Harris. I've been given your number..." I went on to explain my mission.

After a moment's hesitation, Lady Dingdell agreed to do the survey.

While maintaining my new posh voice, I read the first question as quickly as possible. The £2 expenses ever present in my mind.

"You haven't used your in store credit card for over six months," I asked, "Would you mind telling me why?"

"Yes I have." came back the indignant reply. "I bought pan's, yes pans for my daughter at Christmas."

"Oh, I'm sorry, the information I have says you haven't used your card." my B B C voice faded somewhat.

"Yes I jolly well have used it, Neville, Neville, this woman on the phone says we've not use our credit card, find the statements." She commanded of who I have guessing was Lord Dingdell.

"Don't worry..." I tried.

"No, No, there you are, saucepans purchased on the 16th December, I knew it, as well as the hacking jacket I bought for myself at the same time."

How I was supposed to see the statement through the phone, I wasn't sure.

"Plus," she commanded, "I always buy Neville's sock there, don't I Neville?"

A metal picture flashed before me. Lord and Lady Dingdell, maybe in an ermine cloak, Neville dressed in his socks with those sexy suspenders designed to hold men's sock up, Lady Dingdell perhaps with hacking jacket under said cloak, both checking the statement to prove I was lying.

I listened, unable to get a word in edgeways as she reeled off the reason why they maybe hadn't spent as much as in pervious years. They had moved to the country now, the move had been essential. Neville, you see has these tedious but terrible headaches. They were hoping the new glasses may help. However one misses London so much. Their daughter, 'Loop the Loop' or what, ever her name was loved the saucepans, fantastic value. She told her, Mummy their great. Finally drawing breath, Lady Dingdell said she would have to terminate the conversation, lovely as it had been talking to me, as luncheon was now being served. Saying her good byes she genteelly rang off.

I sat staring at the wall. Wondering how it had all gone so horrible wrong. Wasn't conversation a two way thing, maybe not!

Peter put his head round the door of my office, "What was that about?"

"Oh, something to do with some saucepans a hacking jacket and socks." I said shrugging my shoulders.

Undeterred I picked up the phone. The next person was a Mr. Craig Albright. If I was luck he would answer.

Mr Albright insisted from the onset I call him Craig. From his accent he sounded as if his origins were in the East End of London. A bit of a, 'cor blimy' type.

Craig's number was a mobile, so I would have to be fast in my delivery of the questions, so as not to go over the money for my expenses. There was a awful lot of noise going on in the background, causing me to have to repeat some of the questions twice.

"Sorry about the noise luv." Craig shouted down the phone.

"Yeah, sounds a bit busy your end." the B B C voice now lost for ever.

"Yeah." Craig agreed, "We're buying a car, well it's for the Misses, really."

"Lucky her." I smiled.

"Yeah, just wish she'd make up her mind which one she wants," Craig said, "It's down to either the Aston Martin or the Mercedes 230."

"I guess that's a difficult decision to make."

I'd trouble myself, I thought.

"Anyway in answer to your question Shelley," Craig continued, "We haven't used the credit card as we've been out of the county, we live in Mexico for half of the year, but we'll be going there tomorrow to spend a shed load of money, tell them."

I wondered how much a 'shed load' of money would be after buying either a Aston Martin or Mercedes 230. That sort of purchase would clear me out and then some. Craig wasn't showing off, he was just enjoying his money, and why not.

"OK thanks Craig, finally can I ask you the occupation of the chief income earner of the household?"

"Banking." Craig replied.

"Banking, is that you?" I asked

"Yes."

"Are you, a manager?" I questioned.

"No."

"Can I ask your job title, are you a managing director?" I asked.

"No, I own the bank." Craig said as matter of fact.

"Oh." I wrote down owner of bank on the questionnaire, "Thanks enjoy your spending spree."

"Yeah, I'm sure we will sweet heart, nice talking to you." Then he hung up.

Looking at the list of names left to call, I resigned myself to the fact that the £2 expenses, for each phone call was not going to cover the costs. Never mind it was going to be an experience doing this one.

Thank You

Nowadays I feel very lucky. I have a great time doing my job. Not everyone can say that. Of course there are days when it's too cold or even too hot when I think I would rather be doing something else, but what, gardening?

I believe my job has the lot: you meet some of the most interesting people, you meet some very strange people, and then there are the kindest of people whom you feel could even become a friend one day.

It's a job with no one looking over your shoulder. You obviously have to do the job properly or you don't get any more work, but it's not rocket science. It can be challenging.

I have to say a big thank you to all of you I have meet over the years, those I have interviewed who have made me feel welcome or caused me to laugh, or even given me a chapter for this book – those who have made me feel it was a privilege to have been able to spend a few moments with you. To those I've worked with and, I hope, will continue to work with, what can I say? You're great, and it's been fun.

I can't promote this type of work enough, but maybe I shouldn't. People reading this may want to try it and then I would lose out on some work. But as Pamela said, 'It's not for everyone!

Lightning Source UK Ltd.
Milton Keynes UK
172170UK00001B/75/P